11074223

THE OFFICE ENVIRONMENT
Automation's Impact on Tomorrow's Workplace

THE OFFICE ENVIRONMENT
Automation's Impact on Tomorrow's Workplace

Wilbert O. Galitz
President - Galitz, Inc.
St. Charles, Illinois

The second of a four-part study on
"Managing the Office — 1990 and Beyond,"
sponsored in part by a grant from the Olsten Corporation

Administrative Management Society Foundation
2360 Maryland Road, Willow Grove, Pennsylvania 19090

Copyright © 1984 Administrative Management Society Foundation

All rights reserved. No part of this publication may be reproduced, stored in a retrieval system, or transmitted, in any form or by any means, electronic, mechanical, photocopying, recording, or otherwise, without the prior written permission of the publisher. Printed in the United States of America.

ISBN 0-916875-00-8 (softcover)
ISBN 0-916875-01-6 (hardcover)

Other reports in the AMS Foundation's four-part study on "Managing The Office — 1990 and Beyond":

Part One
Human Resources Factors — Spring, 1983

Part Three
Technological Opportunities — Spring, 1985

Part Four
Management Strategies — Spring, 1986

PREFACE AND ACKNOWLEDGEMENTS

The contribution of the office environment to office worker productivity has gone unnoticed or ignored throughout much of the history of the office. The feeling has persisted that the worker will somehow adapt to the existing inadequacies and that the job will get done no matter what. The office worker, typically, has not disappointed those with this view. Applying inherent human flexibility and creativity, the job has usually been accomplished in one way or another.

In recent years, with human productivity waning and technology steadily infiltrating the office, the importance of the office environment and the role it plays in human productivity is becoming much more apparent. Systems that fail to achieve their objectives, health hazard concerns, and the results of research studies are providing dramatic evidence that the office environment fulfills a key role in the successful implementation of the new technologies beginning to shape what is called the office of the future.

This monograph examines the changing office environment and the impact it is having on tomorrow's workplace. Its goal is to aid managers in planning tomorrow's office so that the potential benefits of automation may actually be achieved.

I would like to thank for their support and efforts William Olsten, chairman and chief executive officer of the Olsten Corporation, which partially funded this monograph, the board of trustees of the Administrative Management Society Foundation, and the AMS International Headquarters staff. I would also like to thank the many researchers and practitioners actively involved in the complex and challenging field of the office environment for their contribution to the body of knowledge comprising this monograph. Lastly, I would like to thank my wife, Sharon, for her efforts in editing and typing the final manuscript, and compiling the references.

A portion of the materials in this monograph has been abstracted from my book, *Humanizing Office Automation: The Impact of Ergonomics on Productivity*, recently published by QED Information Sciences, Wellesley, Massachusetts. Those desiring more information about other behavioral or ergonomic aspects of office automation, including the design of systems, hardware, jobs, electronic meetings and other new communication technologies, are invited to read this book.

Wilbert O. Galitz
St. Charles, Illinois
February, 1984

Table of Contents

Introduction 1
Executive Summary 5
Chapter One   The Changing Office 13
    Yesterday's Office 13
    Today's Office 14
    Office Technology and Information 15
    Tomorrow's Office 19
Chapter Two   Automation Concerns 21
    Visual Problems 21
    Postural Problems 28
    Psychosocial Problems 31
    Some Implications 34
    Health Hazards 36
Chapter Three   Workstations 45
    Workstation Problems Caused by the VDT 45
    Workstation Design 47
    A Shaping Influence: Technology 47
    A Shaping Influence: Tasks 47
    A Shaping Influence: Human Needs 51
    Workstation Design Guidelines 54
Chapter Four   Lighting 71
    Illumination Levels 71
    Glare 72
    Natural Light 73
    Visual Display Terminals and Illumination 74
    Task/Ambient Lighting 78
Chapter Five   Acoustics 85
    Acoustical Privacy 88

Noise Control 88
Chapter Six   Office Design and Layout 93
The Open Office 93
Elements 94
Chapter Seven   Telecommuting 105
Advantages 107
Disadvantages 107
Experimental Telecommuting Programs 110
Telecommuting Guidelines and Implications 110
Chapter Eight   Toward the Year 2000 115
Chapter Nine   Conclusion 121

INTRODUCTION

Most of us spend nearly one-third of our adult lives at work. The workplace can be friendly, comfortable, and aesthetically attractive; or it can be inhospitable to one's physical and psychological needs. The experience of many office workers has more often been the latter rather than the former. Poor working environments — bad lighting, noise, inefficiently organized workstations, cluttered desktops, and inadequate chairs — have denied many the chance to use their full potential.

Today, in the midst of the office automation revolution, technology being introduced into the workplace is compounding already-existing environmental problems. It is also unleashing a host of new environmental concerns. Environmental issues have become the subject of frequent and often heated discussion when the topic of office automation is broached in trade publications and the mass media.

Early in the evolution of office automation, some experts recognized that office environments had to be improved if we were to take maximum advantage of automation. These experts felt that environmental design might be the Achilles' heel of the office automation movement unless a conscious effort was made to bring the environment into step with the new technologies. The environmental problems that have surfaced in recent years are mute testimony to this outlook.

Office employees themselves have long been saying that everything is not all right in the workplace. The results of the much-publicized

Steelcase/Louis Harris survey in 1979 detailed a variety of environmental factors that workers felt were most important to doing a job well. Seventy-four percent of the respondents felt they could accomplish more if their working environment were improved. A second, similar survey, published in *Contract* in 1980, revealed that 80 percent of the office workers felt that their job performance had been adversely affected by environmental discomfort. In addition, 84 percent of the managers and executives surveyed also felt that an improved environment would increase the productivity of office workers.

The roots of today's problems are not hard to trace. While human productivity is hard to measure, the costs of walls and desks are not. Cost-effectiveness formulas for workspace design have traditionally emphasized the cost and paid little attention to human effectiveness. Status or rank in an organization has frequently been the key factor in the design process. Implementors of technology have also had little appreciation of the delicate relationship that exists between technology, the environment, and the job itself. A strong and narrow focus on the technology has left little time for addressing environmental considerations. Equipment was simply set on a desk, like a calculator or telephone, and the workers left to fend for themselves as best they could.

As technology moves forward at a breathtaking speed, the environment struggles to keep pace. This approach is no longer practical or wise, and is becoming evident to many businesses today. Technology can no longer be viewed as an end in itself. Office automation, if it is to achieve its lofty promise of improving productivity, must yield the proper blend of technology, people, process, and place. This relationship must be symbiotic rather than reactionary.

This monograph will look at the office environment, a vital ingredient in this symbiotic equation, and how it is being reshaped by the new technology beginning to pervade it. Its objective is to give tomorrow's providers and users of technology the information needed to achieve a true integration of technology and the workplace.

This work begins with a historical review of the traditional office and how it was molded by early technological advancements and processes. It will then look at the effect that adding computer technology has had on today's office, and will unmask problems and concerns. Next, it will examine the environmental components of the office — workstations, lighting, acoustics, and office design and layout. Within each discussion will be a series of design guidelines for effec-

Introduction

tive integration of all pieces. Then it will focus on a new and expanding concept of working — telecommuting or working at home. Finally, it will paint a picture of the office of the 1990s, including potential pitfalls as well as promises.

Executive Summary

In recent years, with human productivity waning and technology steadily infiltrating the office, the importance of the office environment and the role it plays in human productivity is becoming much more apparent. Systems that fail to achieve their objectives, health hazard concerns, and results of research studies are providing dramatic evidence that the office environment fulfills a key role in the successful implementation of the new technologies beginning to shape what is called the office of the future.

This monograph examines the changing office environment and the impact automation is having on tomorrow's workplace. Its goal is to aid managers in planning tomorrow's office so that the potential benefits of automation may actually be achieved. This work summarizes research studies on the effects of environmental factors on office workers. Based on these findings, it pinpoints major concerns and specifically defines environmental ingredients of tomorrow's office, including such elements as lighting, acoustics, climate, workstations, and office layout.

The following presents highlights of this monograph.

The video display terminal (VDT) and the VDT workstation play a role in reported discomforts. A portion of the reported problems appear to be real. The physiology of the human eye and body is not always compatible with the way VDTs are manufactured and installed. VDTs have been manufactured with display characteristics that can fatigue the human eye, and with components arranged to force their users to assume uncomfortable, constrained, and fatiguing postures. VDTs have also been installed in offices in a haphazard way with little thought to good viewing and operating conditions.

Use of VDTs need not be physically fatiguing, however, as evidenced by the people and studies that report no problems. A properly designed VDT and good work environment, while probably not totally devoid of discomforts in today's state of the art, can be made much more comfortable to work with than is commonly the case. Solutions to problems, however, cannot be accomplished by independently addressing the equipment and environment.

Job content also plays a significant role in reported discomforts. Reports of physical ailments can be influenced by the content of the job being performed. Some studies have found higher incidences of physical complaints among clerical users than among professional users of VDTs. The job content of professional users included flexibility in accomplishing goals, control over tasks, utilization of experience and education, and satisfaction and pride in an end product, the kinds of qualities missing from many clerical tasks.

Thus the impact of the job, and the design of the system, have a much larger impact on satisfaction and work stress than many early researchers suspected. The psychosocial needs can overshadow physical needs in a variety of human experiences.

Length of working time plays a role in reported discomforts. It has been found that as the amount of working time at various VDT jobs increases, so does the percentage of workers expressing psychosocial problems. Shorter time periods at VDTs provide opportunities to rest muscles and permit a greater variety in movements and tasks. Studies have yet to be made on optimum time periods but observation indicates that two hours or less a day at the VDT relieves many of the physical problems.

Individual differences play a role in susceptibility to discomfort. No two people are alike. Human physiques, traits, and sensitivities are distributed along the normal distribution curve. The viewing angle of a VDT located in a standardized position may be proper for one person but not for another. One person may perceive display flicker while a second does not in an identical viewing condition. Even the effect of job-related frustrations on people varies. Solutions must consider individual differences; variable opinions and responses are the norm.

Possible adverse health effects associated with VDT use include

reports of unusually high numbers of miscarriages, birth defects and eye cataracts. In reaction to these concerns, a number of studies of the radiation emission qualities of VDTs have been performed by a variety of governmental and nongovernmental organizations around the world. Based on the results of these studies, and the findings of their own study, the authors of the Environmental Health Directorate report (1983) conclude: "There is no reason for any person, male or female, young or old, pregnant or not, to be concerned about radiation health effects from VDTs." Statements like this, however, will probably not end the controversy. We must continue to search for answers that assure everyone that the accelerating use of VDTs is a safe path to follow.

We need to continue the research needed to establish cause and effects while at the same time assuring that VDTs are used properly within the limits of today's knowledge.

Workstation design has become more complex due to the incorporation of the VDT. The VDT has caused awkward terminal operating positions, lost workspace, and inefficient workspace organization. To counter these, and provide an efficient working environment, a host of new considerations must be addressed. Workstation design must incorporate the demands of technology, the tasks to be performed, and various human needs. Providing for human needs involves consideration of both biological needs (body dimensions, sensory, and ambient), and psychological needs (intellectual, social, motivational, and aesthetic). Recognizing the increasingly complex and individualized nature of workstation design, the office furniture industry is moving to a systems approach, involving such elements as task/ambient lighting, component furniture systems, modular storage, and easily adjustable components. Furthermore, the dramatic increase in the variety of elements and services that support a VDT (such as lighting, telephone and data communication cables) will ultimately make workstations more built-in and fixed in location.

Attention to the lighting needs of workers at office systems is now extremely important. Serious attention to lighting is warranted by the impact it can have on worker productivity and health. The increasing complexity of office lighting also requires greater involvement of lighting consultants, since proceeding in ignorance may cause more harm than good. In sum, task/ambient lighting can help solve office lighting problems posed by VDTs. Extreme care must be taken, however, to provide a quality solution. It is important to avoid shadows as well as glare, bright and dim spots, poorly directed light, and similar conditions.

An office layout should optimize the flow of work among various departments and people. It should also minimize movement and sound distractions caused by people going about their activities. The following principles should determine office layouts.
- Keep people close to those with whom they must frequently communicate.
- Keep files and other references close to the people who use them.
- Keep people who have many outside visitors close to the work area entrance.
- Common destinations (toilets, elevators, photocopy machines, and so on) should be close together and accessible by direct routes.
- Workstations should be away from sources of intermittent sounds and areas of frequent conversations.

Toward the Year 2000

Human factors and ergonomic considerations will achieve ever-increasing importance in future environmental design as awareness of their contribution to greater human productivity grows. That this is happening is evidenced by the fact that four of the top five critical human resource problems identified in the first monograph in this series are people-related and can be addressed through application of human factors/ergonomic design principles. That this is happening is also evidenced by the contents of this monograph.

Information. Previously scattered information will be electronically consolidated, thereby reducing the clutter of the workstation. Information will be more accessible to all. Paper will not entirely disappear, however.

Technology. Miniaturization of technology will continue. The bulky cathode ray tube (CRT) will gradually be replaced by flat-panel displays offering compactness, increased mobility, and the capability of being built into the workstation. Advances in display support electronics will yield improved resolution, color, split-screen capabilities and three-dimensional perspectives. Larger displays will also be available, permitting the presentation of more information at one time.

The typewriter-type keyboard will remain a primary human-computer interface mechanism, but touch-panel displays and pointers such as the mouse and trackballs will have widespread use. Voice recognition and synthesis will be viable in a variety of applications.

Workstations will be more built-in and fixed in location. The next major restructuring of the workstation will occur as the components of the computer interface system are included within the working surfaces themselves. Terminals will cease to be instruments supported by a surface, but will become part of the work surface. In some ways the workstation may become one large terminal.

Another technology on the horizon will soon have a large impact on workstation design — talking computers. Voice communications between people and systems will usher in a whole new era of acoustical concerns and solutions as the office din increases while workstation size decreases as a result of more costly office space. The creative worker, while being freed from the mechanics of interfacing with a keyboard, will be exposed to the distractions caused by an escalating major noise source in the office, the human voice.

Ultimately, an effective workstation design is going to require even closer cooperation among all interested parties — furniture manufacturers, terminal manufacturers, facility managers, and computer users. Those who are not yet talking to each other had better start quickly.

The workstation of tomorrow will be smaller. Electronic information consolidation will eliminate the need for large areas to store information on paper and the materials needed for paper handling. At the same time, however, greater visual and auditory privacy will be needed. Noise created by equipment and voice computer interaction will create severe acoustical problems. Display terminals and other technologies will be incorporated within the workstation itself. The surface of the desk and workstation walls will become control and viewing surfaces. The chair may also contain fingertip controls. The office workstation and the airplane cockpit may bear some resemblance to each other.

Comfort in working will be achieved through intelligent chairs and desks. Desk heights and angles will be modified through the simple touch of a button. Desired configurations will be remembered by the desk's electronics and changed as the needs of a person change. The chair may actually configure itself to its occupant through analysis of weight distribution.

Office buildings as we know them today will continue to operate. A reduction in paper and paper filing requirements, and more people working at home or in satellite offices, will diminish space requirements, however. Offices and conference rooms will also still exist. Electronic meetings are a poor substitute for a variety of communications requiring interpersonal interaction. These will best be addressed by people facing people.

Tomorrow's office will provide a computer utility akin to that provided by the electric and telephone companies. A variety of computing services will be available as easily as turning on a light switch.

The technology of tomorrow raises some critical environmental issues that must be addressed. Each will have a significant impact on the well-being of the office worker and the organization. These issues pertain to noise, electronic social isolation, and health.

Noise. As human-computer interaction methods change, and voice communication assumes a greater role in the dialogue, a new dimension will be added to the office din. Talking people and talking computers will be an even greater source of distraction. An office acoustics program will be necessary to keep sound and noise levels within a range that is comfortable for performing human office activities. Those levels should eliminate distractions, allow good hearing and provide speech privacy.

Tomorrow's office must provide the proper social environment as well. As we direct more and more of our attention to the computer and structure our workstations around it, the office design must still foster and encourage the human-to-human interactions so vital to us all. The environment must provide the degree of privacy demanded by the new technologies while at the same time not inhibit the necessary face-to-face communications of people with other people.

Tomorrow's jobs must not be made too comfortable. Organization of the items comprising the workstation and the job themselves must have within them the requirement for a certain degree of physical movement. The challenge will be to stay on the right side of the line separating healthy diversity from fatigue. Workstation component adjustability will be a key element in achieving this objective. Being able to easily assume a variety of different working postures during the day will provide needed exercise for a range of muscles. Health clubs or exercise rooms may also become integral parts of the office. The coffee break, now used to mentally and physically recharge fatigued minds and bodies, may be supplemented by the exercise break to replenish stiff and rigid bodies.

Lastly, legislation may impose an unnecessary financial burden on the occasional users of VDTs. Occasional users are not subjected to all

Executive Summary

the problems described here; to impose solutions to nonproblems is not cost effective. Furthermore, state or Federally mandated requirements necessitate monitoring mechanisms to assure company compliance with the law. This results in tax dollars being spent for solutions of dubious long-term value to companies and society.

Psychosocial problems and the physical ailments associated with posture and vision cannot really be neatly divided into separate categories. Nor can the effects of the hardware, the system, the environment, and an organization's management. The worker, too, must be looked upon not just as one but as many with a variety of needs, interests, attitudes and susceptibilities.

A tangible benefit of increased attention to the environment will be increased productivity. Intangible benefits include decreased absenteeism, improved job satisfaction and morale, and lowered workers' compensation claims and costs. Humanizing the workplace can also serve as a proactive response to the charges by interest groups and organized labor about the health and safety of working with VDTs.

We must not lose sight of the fact, however, that the road to successful office system implementation requires complete harmony of the worker, the organization, and the technology. The product of our efforts must result in a condition where jobs, computer systems, equipment, the work environment, and motivations and psychological needs of the workers are properly woven into a whole office fabric. Then the process of change must be carefully managed. The results of our efforts will be no stronger than the weakest thread.

Chapter One
THE CHANGING OFFICE

The office is a recent innovation in the history of mankind. In its short existence, however, it has undergone radical technological changes that have shaped and reshaped the jobs and working environment of its inhabitants. The promise for tomorrow is even more dramatic and accelerated change.

Yesterday's Office

The office of the 1800s was very different from that which exists today. Most organizations were small and occupied a single location. The few employees located outside the office were usually agents marketing the company's products elsewhere. The bulk of written communication occurred between the company and the outside world.

In the early office, internal communications were generally face-to-face, and internal written documents were infrequent. Storage for written communications usually consisted of pigeonholes and rolltop desks and boxes or drawers in which paper was stored flat. Outgoing correspondence was copied by pressing it between the dampened tissue leaves of a bound press book. Searching for correspondence required knowing the approximate dates of creation and the location of frequently moved storage boxes. Since incoming and outgoing correspondence was stored in a different manner, it was impossible to retrieve all on the same subject at a single try. "Technological support" for yesterday's office was initiated with the invention and mass production of the typewriter in the 1870s, followed shortly by the telephone.

In the late 1800s companies began to grow larger and more complex. The volume of external correspondence ballooned, and the need for internal correspondence became obvious. Two more technological innovations were needed to cope with changing needs.

The first innovation involved a method for vertically storing information to make it more accessible. In 1876 vertical card files were created for libraries, and in 1893 vertical office files were introduced by a library supply company. Drawers eliminated the need to unstack boxes, and vertical positioning of their contents enabled them to be searched without removing the contents.

The second innovation was a way of producing loose, rather than bound, copies of documents. This need was satisfied by Edison's invention of the mimeograph machine about 1870, and the creation of carbon paper, which achieved widespread use shortly after 1900. Combined with vertical filing, these reproduction methods enabled incoming and outgoing correspondence to be easily stored and retrieved together. It created an *organization memory* independent of the memory of the people who stored the information.

Vertical filing created a revolution in offices. In the first two decades of this century, a dramatic increase in internal memoranda occurred. Standard formats were devised and various indexing schemes developed. Filing areas sprang up in all kinds of organizations and departments.

The elements of this early office — the desks, chairs, files, lights, floor plans, kinds of job, and so forth — evolved to expedite the flow of paper through the system. Since paper was handled manually, control over the form and pace of the information flow and job performance rested primarily with the worker. The design of the office components were standardized, reflecting primarily engineering and manufacturing considerations. The modern office had arrived — or so it seemed.[1]

Today's Office

The seeds for today's office were sown in the late 1930s and 1940s with the invention of the photocopier and computer. In the 1960s the development of xerography began to unleash tons of paper into the

The Changing Office

office at the push of a button. In the 1960s and 1970s the computer began providing a viable, alternative means of storing information by permitting it to be done electronically. It also made possible the creation and transmission of information electronically and reduced the time in which tasks could be performed from hours to seconds.

The computer's invasion of the office has been meteoric. Various estimates indicate that one in every seven to ten white-collar workers today interact with a computer in one way or another. Some occupations, such as banking and insurance, will find 90 percent of their tasks accomplished electronically before the decade is over.

The office in which automation is firmly trying to entrench itself, however, has solid roots. Since the revolutionary changes around the turn of this century, the office has been characterized by stability and slow change. It is a nebulous environment of human interactions, communications, and rigid habits, and its pulse is difficult to take.

Furthermore, while office costs are increasing at a rate of 12 to 15 percent a year, the typical office employee utilizes only 40 percent of his or her potential. Many of the office's occupants, especially managers and professionals, have traditionally been told only what to do and how to do it. They have tended to develop highly personalized ways of working.

As far as design, today's office elements are primarily carryovers from the earlier era when manufacturing considerations prevailed. It is not unusual to see desks and chairs from the 1950s in today's office.

The work ethic of the modern office worker is also changing. The desire for material possessions is expanding to include psychological concerns. Today's office employees are much more concerned with quality of worklife and humanization of the work environment. Interesting and meaningful work is a main goal. Variety is preferred to routine, and informality to structure. The authority of management is being questioned, and participation in decisions affecting a person's work is becoming increasingly important.[2]

Office Technology and Information

Today, the visible symbol of office automation is the equipment or hardware itself. In the early days of computing, the standard typewriter-type keyboard was the means by which people could interface with the computer. This keyboard was familiar, contained all the necessary keys and characters to input information, and was flexible and versatile. Paired with this keyboard was a hard-copy printer. This printer enabled a person to view inputs that had been constructed and was a mechanism with which computer outputs could be written. While slow and requiring frequent, highly-structured inputs, these devices satisfied many of the needs of the technicians who were the most common computer users.

A significant advancement in the adaption of people to computers occurred when the typewriter keyboard was paired with the cathode ray tube (CRT) display. Mechanical restrictions were removed and the speed of interaction was dramatically increased as alphanumeric information, lines, and graphics were presented on screen at electronic speeds. User creation of inputs was also greatly simplified and quickened as electronic editing became possible.

The earliest users of these new devices, now commonly called the visual display termnal or VDT, were mostly military. Toward the mid-1960s commercial applications began to surface. Pioneer users included national airlines. A certain amount of human engineering of these devices occurred as attempts were made to make the displays legible, readable and comfortable, and the keyboard touch characteristics compatible with human needs.

The 1970s saw the introduction of new generations of display terminals with more sophisticated capabilities. Character resolution improved and techniques for displaying information greatly expanded. Whereas older alphanumeric terminals simply displayed a character of one size and brightness, newer terminals possessed such techniques as two levels of character brightness, upper and lower case characters, and light characters on dark backgrounds as well as the reverse. The 1970s also saw a movement toward better human engineering as keyboards began to be detached from the display.

The VDT of the 1980s has benefitted from even better human engineering, as the problems and concerns with VDT use escalated. Rotatable and tiltable display screens and glare-reducing filters are but a few of the innovations. However, while the VDT of today has changed quite a bit from its ancestors, it is still a fairly large device consuming a significant amount of desk space.

It is expected that CRT display technology will remain the dominant person-computer interface method at least through the remainder of the decade. Capabilities will continue to increase through improved support electronics. Advancements will occur in even more improved resolution, and the addition of color, split-screen capabilities and three-dimensional perspectives.

As the information in today's office moves from a paper-based to an electronic-based medium, the characteristics of the information are changing in both substance and style. The visual display terminal possesses many characteristics that are almost the opposite of paper, as shown in Table 1-1 and highlighted below.[3]

Display characteristics. Information displayed on paper is legible and readable, based upon years of research toward developing a quality product. The matte surface of paper diffuses reflected light, scarcely affecting the quality of the material presented. Paper-based

---

Table 1-1
**General Characteristics of
Two Visual Display Media**

Paper/Hardcopy

- Dark characters on a light background
- Continuous line characters
- Matte surface
- Horizontal plane
- Manual input
- Easy to handle
- Perceptually permanent
- Data stored physically
- Information presented simultaneously

Electronic/VDT

- Light characters on a dark background
- Dot-matrix characters
- Reflective surface
- Vertical plane
- Keyboard input
- Difficult to manipulate
- Perceptually transient
- Data stored electronically
- Information presented serially

information may be read under a variety of lighting conditions. By contrast, VDT characters are luminous and often of a dot-matrix construction. The character image may be blurred by dust on the VDT screen or by reflections from overhead lights or windows. In general, reading information on a display screen imposes greater visual demands on a person than does reading information on a piece of paper.

Viewing plane. Papers are normally read horizontally, such as resting on a desk top. They may be read vertically, however, by physically raising the paper to a position perpendicular to the eye. VDTs are normally read in a vertical plane since internal mechanics and concerns with light reflections permit little flexibility.

Kind of input. Papers are normally completed by hand, and VDTs through use of a keyboard. Writing skills are far more common than the keying skills. When writing, a person's eyes follow the hands, providing immediate feedback. When keying, the hands operate in a different visual plane than that of the information display. Therefore, keying is a more complex visual motor task.

Handling characteristics. Paper can easily be manipulated to move it into a comfortable viewing position. It can be held forward, backward, tilted, placed on the desk, or placed or held at arm's length. VDTs, on the other hand, are difficult to move. Viewing angles and distances can usually be changed only by posture changes of the viewer, such as leaning forward, backward, or to the side.

Information permanence. A hard copy is relatively permanent. Information seldom disappears from paper. Paper can, however, be misplaced or misfiled. Information on a VDT screen can disappear as a result of a power interruption, computer malfunction, or the inadvertent pressing of a wrong key. The perceptual and physical permanence of information can affect the way people think and feel about it. The physical permanence and control of paper is usually preferred to the transience and lack of control of the computer.

Information presentation. Display of information on a VDT is limited by the boundaries or size of the display area. Often information must be presented serially as a string of snapshots viewed in sequence. Comparisons of information displayed on different screens is difficult. To do so requires an exceptional memory or, more often, paper-and-pencil notes. The breadth of display of paper information is only restricted by the physical size of the work area.

This seemingly simple change from paper to electronics is having profound consequences on office personnel and the office environment. Since the VDT will remain the primary person-computer interface mechanism into the early 1990s, it must be considered the foundation in environmental planning for the time being. Problems in its use, and guidelines for its effective integration into the office, will be described in the chapters that follow.

Tomorrow's Office

Other dramatic changes are on the horizon. A significant reduction in terminal size will occur as flat panel electronic displays with superior resolution become more widely available in the next five to ten years. This will permit incorporation of the display within the workstation, instead of necessitating that it be placed on the desk surface as is usually done today.

Another innovation to have a profound impact on the office environment will be more widespread application of voice communication with a computer. When it becomes practical (estimates range from soon to never) it will unleash a host of acoustical problems that must be addressed. (A look at the office of the more distant future will be found in Chapter Eight.)

NOTES

1. "Historical Lessons for the Automated Office," by M. Lynne Markus and JoAnn Yates, *Computer Decisions,* June, 1982, pp. 116-121.
2. "The Office of 1990 - Human Resources," by Joseph McKendrick, *Management World,* January 1982, p. 14.
3. "Automation, Ergonomics and Offices: Evolution or Revolution?" by T.J. Springer, *Journal of Information Management,* Fall, 1982.

Chapter Two
AUTOMATION CONCERNS

The introduction of computer technology into the office, while producing many benefits, has unleashed a wave of growing concern over potential negative side effects of working at VDTs. Concerns over such issues as visual and postural problems, increased work stress, reduction in the quality of working life, lost jobs, and health hazards have created a storm of rhetoric that has spawned a growing number of studies around the world.

The realities of automation's side effects are increasingly difficult to pinpoint due to the enormity and complexity of the issues. These issues are also being clouded by those whose interests may be more political than humanitarian. The safest and most practical approach is to take one step backward and look at the entire situation objectively. The more significant considerations should then emerge and the risk of bogging down in detail should lessen. The following reviews significant research and considerations to be kept in mind in making a move to automation.

Visual Problems

Numerous field studies in recent years have uncovered a variety of complaints about eye troubles associated with using visual display terminals (for example, Crane 1979, Meyer *et al* 1979, Hultgreen & Knave 1974, Elias *et al* 1980, Smith *et al* 1981, Läubli *et al* 1980,

Nishiyama *et al* 1983, and Ong 1983 — see end of chapter for specific references.) The most commonly reported visual discomforts are eye strain, burning and/or irritated eyes, and blurred or double vision. Dainoff *et al* (1981) found a moderate but significant correlation between visual discomforts and time spent using the VDT.

Buttressing these field studies are a number of experimental studies addressing the eye mechanism itself. Haider *et al* (1975, 1980) found a reduction in the eye's visual acuity after three to four hours of continuous work on a VDT. Gunnarsson and Soderberg (1980) have found that the near point of accommodation and convergence moves away during the workday, and this effect is greater for VDT work than non-VDT work. Mourant *et al* (1979) found that the time to visually focus on a far point increased as a function of time using a VDT. These studies also reported a tendency for subjective symptoms of visual fatigue to be correlated with the physiological changes measured.

Other studies, however, have reported no problems, or at least no differences in reported eye discomforts between VDT and non-VDT users. Falling into this category are studies by DeGroot (1981), Starr *et al* (1982), Hedman *et al* (1983), and Sauter (1983). Many of the studies reporting problems have also been criticized for methodological deficiencies (Starr *et al,* 1982 and Schurick *et al* 1982). Such deficiencies have included failure to use control groups, improper subject selection, failure to allow for other influences such as those of the task or workstation, and failure to control emotional issues involving sensitive concerns, such as health and job security, which could bias the results.

However, all researchers agree that the visual discomforts of VDT work are transient, not permanent. What then can we conclude? Before venturing an opinion, let us examine the source of concern: the human eye.

The eye is much like a camera. Entering light passes through an opening in the iris called the pupil and is focused by the lens onto an area of the retina called the fovea. There it is translated into electrical impulses and transmitted by the optic nerve to the brain. The visual system is controlled by a series of muscles that work in opposition to one another.

One set of muscles controls the shape of the lens which brings images at varying distances into sharp focus (accommodation and convergence). A second set of muscles in the iris controls the amount of light entering the eye (adaptation). With light stimulation the retina gradually loses its sensitivity, while in the absence of light it gradually recovers it. While normal viewing occurs in the center of the retina, incidental light is absorbed throughout it. Excessive light in the periphery of the field of vision, then, can cause some light adaptation throughout the retina and subsequent degradation of visual ability.

The eye perceives differences by detecting differences in brightness or color within the visual field. With little or no contrast, no edge is perceived, but as contrast increases, edge perception improves until finally additional contrast no longer helps. At a certain point extreme brightness contrast begins to impair visual performance by creating a contrast glare. Luminance brightness relationships must, therefore, be kept within narrow limits.

Another series of muscles gives the brain a more reliable picture by providing slightly different views through quick small movements of the eye. These movements, called rapid saccadic movements, compensate for the tendency of the retina's cells to tire.

Problems with the human optic system may be either psysiological or induced by the environment. Environmental conditions that force extensive use of eye muscles can cause fatigue. The muscles' function will be impaired until they have had time to rest and recover. Excessive muscle fatigue lowers a person's visual skills, and tasks then become more difficult, requiring more effort and concentration.

Physiologically, the lens may have an improper shape, which results in an out-of-focus image being projected onto the retina. This is commonly called nearsightedness or farsightedness. With age the lens loses its elasticity, thereby reducing the range of eye focus that can be achieved. With age the lens also loses its transparency, thereby reducing visual acuity. These physiological problems are commonly corrected through use of eyeglasses or contact lenses.

Discomfort can have a major impact on reading performance. If a display is irritating or difficult to read, reading performance will probably suffer (Snyder and Taylor 1979, and Vartebedian 1971).

Many attempts have been made to find objective criteria to measure visual fatigue. That is, is there some objective measure such as blink rate, pupil diameter, or eye fixations that correlates with a measurable discomfort symptom? So far, efforts to determine this have been unsuccessful. Human feelings remain the primary descriptive source of information.

Examination of research results, knowledge of the haphazard ways in which VDTs have been installed in offices around the world, and a comparison of the physical attributes of displays with the functioning of the human eye, lead to the inescapable conclusion that something is wrong. The evidence is too strong to suggest otherwise. But it would be as unreasonable to conclude that VDTs cause eye discomfort as it would be to conclude that they do not cause eye discomfort. To reach one or the other conclusion would be like saying that reading a magazine does or does not cause eye discomfort. A magazine with clear legible characters being viewed under the proper amount of light normally yields little if any eye discomfort. The same magazine read under the harsh glare of a desk lamp, or on a moving train with poor springs, or in an automobile being driven through flickering tree shadows on a bright sunny day would probably result in considerable discomfort. Whether the magazine was the first or last in the press run and/or has dark or light print will also influence the degree of reading comfort.

No two VDTs are exactly alike. Design characteristics vary, the environments in which they are used vary, and the tasks being performed vary. Thus it is no surprise that the results of various studies are confusing. Like reading a magazine, VDT work can be made more difficult or easier. If a fault exists, it is because the breadth and complexity of the issues have not been understood, and too much faith has been placed in the inherent adaptability of people to technology. In some cases bad judgments have been made.

Based on the physiology of the eye, there are some characteristics of VDTs and their environment that can contribute to eye discomfort. Table 2-1 summarizes these factors, which are described further in the following.

Excessive luminance contrast in the visual field. Large brightness contrast between display screen, source documents, windows and lights may strain the eye's adaptive mechanism. A bright light source close to the line of sight can cause the iris muscle to open and close repeatedly, as can frequent eye movements between a dark display screen and a brightly lit source document. Research performed by TUV Reinland and reported in *Mini-Micro Systems* found 8,000 to 25,000 eye movements occur between a display screen and source documents over an eight-hour day.

Large brightness contrast in the field of vision can cause the eye to adapt to the brightest source. If the bright source is in the background, the eyes may adjust to the background and make reading the

Automation Concerns 25

Table 2-1
Potential Causes of Visual Discomfort Associated with Using Visual Display Terminals

Equipment/Environment

- Excessive luminance contrast in the visual field
- Variable focus distance in the visual field
- Screen reflections
- Oscillating display character brightness (flicker)

Equipment

- Low contrast between display characters and background
- Excessive display character brightness
- Low display character stability
- Poor display character sharpness
- Poor display character legibility
- Divergent light wavelengths (color)

Human

- Uncorrected eye defects
- Eyeglasses

display difficult. Several studies reporting visual discomfort found excessive luminance contrast ratios in the visual field (Hultgreen and Knave 1974, Luäbli *et al* 1982, Stammerjohn *et al* 1981, and Coe *et al* 1980).

Variable focus distance in the visual field. Muscles may tire if the eyes have to converge and diverge repeatedly in looking rapidly between objects at different distances. This is a special problem for older people whose refocusing distance time has degraded. Rapid changes in visual focal points may occur thousands of times daily if information sources are positioned at different viewing distances.

Screen reflections. Display screens frequently have highly reflective glass surfaces that reflect light from such environmental sources as windows, lights, and other bright surfaces. When these reflections diminish the contrast between characters and background, visual acuity drops and reading difficulties occur. In some cases the reflected light is bright enough to cause glare. Almost all studies reporting visual discomfort found screen reflections to be serious problems.

Oscillating display character brightness (flicker). To maintain a constant display image, a VDT's phosphor must be continually refreshed. If it falls below a certain level, the oscillation is perceived as a flickering light. Flicker has adverse effects because it overloads the adaptation mechanism of the eye. Little is known about the effects of non-visible flicker, or non-perceived oscillation of VDTs. But it is known that non-perceived oscillation of fluorescent lights may cause complaints of irritated eyes from some people working under them. There are reasons to assume that non-visible oscillation in VDTs may also have adverse effects on the retina of very sensitive persons (Grandjean, updated).

The degree of perceived flicker depends upon some physical characteristics of the VDT itself as well as some environmental conditions. Generally, flicker is more noticeable with:
- lower phosphor refresh rates;
- shorter phosphor persistence rates;
- higher display character brightness;
- lower display background brightness; and
- lower room illumination levels.

Low contrast between display characters and background. The characters displayed on some VDTs are simply not very bright. In this case visual acuity drops and reading difficulties occur.

Excessive display character brightness. High levels of character brightness can create contrast or direct glare. Bright images can cause the characters to be indistinct and also cause reading problems.

Low display character stability, sharpness and legibility. Characters which "swim," are fuzzy, or are poorly designed also stress the eye's accommodating power.

Divergent light wavelengths (color). The eye refracts light of different wavelengths (color) in different ways. Light simultaneously entering the eye from sources with widely divergent color compositions (dual-source light) cannot be brought into simultaneous sharp focus. The eye must adapt individually to each light source to clarify each image. Eye irritation may result when frequent adaptations are necessary. Colors close to the end of the visual spectrum create the worst problems.

Uncorrected eye defects. People generally do not take care of their eyes as they should. It is variously estimated that from one-third to

Automation Concerns

one-half of all people have an uncorrected eye defect of one kind or another. Above the age of forty, eye defects become the rule rather than the exception. Wearing glasses or contact lenses is not always the solution. One study of clerical and administrative workers found that 37 percent of the eyeglass wearers were in need of a new prescription (Cakir *et al* 1979). For those with uncorrected eye defects, working at what may be a visually demanding task will certainly not make the job any easier. The result will make existing poor conditions worse.

Eyeglasses. As the eye lens gradually begins to stiffen around the age of forty, and refocusing becomes more difficult, eyeglasses are often needed for normal reading. Reading glasses are set for a normal reading distance of about 12 to 15 inches. VDTs are often read at distances of 18 inches or more, thereby lowering visual acuity. Continued stiffening of the eye lens with advancing years often results in the need for an additional set of glasses for long-distance viewing. The common solution is a pair of double-lens glasses (bifocals), the lower portion used for near viewing and the upper for distance. Again, these are not set for normal VDT viewing distances, resulting in the same problem.

Current evidence indicates that visual discomfort associated with working at VDTs can be attributed to a combination of three factors: improperly designed display units, unsuitable lighting conditions, or the task itself.

Improperly designed display units take their toll on the accommodation and adaptation mechanisms of the eye. Läubli *et al* (1982) found significant differences in eye discomfort when comparing terminals possessing good character sharpness, high character stability, and low degree of oscillation with those lacking these qualities. The better-designed terminals gave fewer problems.

However, many characteristics of the display screen cannot be considered independent of the environment in which they are used. Perception of flicker and luminance contrast ratios both depend somewhat on one another. Some environmental factors may act independently of the equipment, of course. A severe direct glare source may be almost totally debilitating, taking its toll on the accommodation and adaptation mechanisms of the eye.

Finally, the task being performed may cause reported visual discomfort. Thousands of eye movements a day between a display screen and surrounding source materials are likely to be the result of a poorly designed task or series of tasks. Such a situation can only magnify any equipment/environmental problems that may exist. The relationship of visual discomfort to one's job has further critical implications that will be discussed later.

It is evident that there is still much to learn. The depth and complexity of the considerations yield no easy answers. What is needed is a more comprehensive and dynamic model in which the specific attributes of the visual environment are linked to the specific aspects of the visual function. It is also evident that individual differences play a significant role in the perception of discomfort. Some people find a situation uncomfortable that others can tolerate. Ultimate answers must satisfy a range of people. Until this is achieved, if it ever is achieved, we must use the knowledge available today to create as fine a viewing environment as possible.

What is known, if consciously applied, can eliminate or alleviate much of the reported discomforts. Later chapters will address these solutions. The benefits, in addition to the obvious physical one for VDT users, can also be measured in performance. Wodka (1982) has derived a formula for determining the reading rate of VDT displays based upon calculations that the Illuminating Engineering Society Research Institute has derived for calculating changes in industrial and paper-oriented office tasks. Using this formula, Ryburg (1981) has estimated that VDT reading speeds and task accuracy in a large office studied can be improved three to seven percent by establishing proper lighting for VDT use.

Postural Problems

Like visual discomfort, innumerable studies have uncovered reports of postural problems associated with using VDTs. In addition to those previously referenced, further problems have been uncovered by Ferguson (1971), Hünting et al (1980), and Maeda (1977) in using other office equipment. The most commonly reported problems are pains in the neck, shoulder, back, arms, and hands. As in the case of vision, not all studies have yielded problems (Starr et al 1982), and many of the studies have been criticized for methodological deficiencies.

While eyestrain may be a more sensitive issue, postural problems can be more serious in the long run. The body muscles are sensitive tissues. If underused, they will atrophy. If overloaded or improperly used, they may fatigue, suffer temporary damage, or even suffer permanent damage. Fatigued muscles will impair performance; dam-

Automation Concerns

aged muscles may prevent a task from being performed.

Atrophy is prevented by building variety into manual tasks. Astronauts in the confines of a space capsule are forced to reach for some controls and materials to provide needed muscle exercise. Muscle fatigue is reduced by letting a person assume relaxing and comfortable positions, and not forcing a set of muscles to undergo continuous activity.

Again, the depth and breadth of complaints must lead one to the conclusion that something is amiss. To understand more fully, let us look at the office worker's desk.

Before the use of visual display terminals, the office desk was characterized by a collection of working materials (forms, files, books, manuals, etc.), tools (pencils, ruler, stapler, etc.), and storage facilities (drawers, shelves, etc.). Commonly shared items (file cabinets, photocopy machines, etc.) were a short walk away. Most items on the desk were movable and portable by the desk's occupant. A comfortable working position could be created by arranging the items in a manner deemed most convenient by the worker. Changes in position could easily be accomplished. A manual, for example, could be read flat on the desk surface, held at an angle perpendicular to the desk surface, on one's lap, or even lie on the floor if desired. In essence the worker controlled the working environment, easily modifying it to achieve maximum comfort. Periodic movements throughout the work area were often required and changes in seating posture were easily accomplished.

Gradually, however, working materials, tools, and storage facilities have been replaced by VDTs. The VDT is large, bulky, and difficult to move. It is placed on desks intended to support the manual materials that it replaces. Location of the display screen and keyboard is generally fixed, often in a location far less than optimum for human comfort. VDT users have been forced to adapt their posture to the rigid requirements imposed by the machine. As more and more tasks are internalized within the system, the diversity of movements to accomplish a job are diminished. A variety of muscular movements are replaced by one — the keystroke.

Muscle fatigue and injuries associated with the use of VDTs can be attributed to several factors: awkward posture, constrained posture, and repetitive movements. Those who wear bifocal eyeglasses may have to assume an awkward posture in order to read a display screen. They must tilt their heads backward and incline their torso forward to bring the image into focus through the reading lens.

A person is linked to the VDT through both the keyboard and the screen. Both head and hands must be kept in practically a fixed position, with the remainder of the body, neck, shoulders, trunk and arms following suit. The keying and viewing tasks constrain both posture and movement. If the position assumed is not comfortable, the problems are magnified.

Repetitive movement injuries are caused by repeated rapid movements, not necessarily involving heavy loads or long duration. Such injuries often take the form of tenosynovitis and tendinitis. In a study of the data entry department of a large Australian bank, Teniswood (1982) found 20 cases of compensable tenosynovitis over a four-year period. These injuries occurred in a staff of about 90 people who performed predominantly right-handed keying tasks at rates of 16,000 keystrokes per hour.

Discomfort and injuries of this type cannot be attributed solely to VDTs in the workplace, however. Back trouble has been a hazard facing typists and machine operators for years. Patkin (1983) reports treating an office worker for a hand injury caused by improper use of a pencil. The problem was pressing the pencil too firmly on the paper. The cure was not to press so hard!

Unlike vision, the components of comfortable posture are better understood. Factors which can contribute to postural discomfort include the following.

Improper viewing angles. Display screens are often set too high, with the results that the normal downward inclination of the head is not achieved. This increases the strain on neck muscles. Screen viewing problems created by display and environmental deficiencies often force people to assume awkward body positions in order to read the display. This can lead to postural problems.

Poor chairs. Proper chair height and back support is a necessity for sedentary activities. Without it, the muscles surrounding the spinal cord may be strained and the delicate ligaments and tissues around the vertebrae may be pinched.

High rates of input. High input rates force the maintenance of constrained positions for extended periods of time. They can also lead to repetitive movement injuries.

There is reasonable agreement on the desired posture of a seated person using a VDT. (Guidelines will be presented in Chapter Three.) The problem of high input rates is not an environmental problem. It is a function of the design of the job and the equipment used.

Psychosocial Problems

A third area of concern centers around a person's psychological reactions to automation. Limited research evidence indicates that some users of VDTs are more likely to show higher stress symptoms than their colleagues who do not use VDTs. Factors measured include anxiety, depression, irritability, boredom, inner security, anger, confusion, and general fatigue. Complementing the research data is a growing number of voices expressing fears about the direction automation is steering the quality of worklife, and the effect this is having on the psychological wellbeing of the worker. Factors suggested as potential causes of work stress are summarized in Table 2-2 and described below.

Rigid work procedures. Rigid work procedures do not permit any flexibility in how a task is accomplished. Cohen *et al* (1982) found rigid work procedures were one of the distinguishing features when comparing two kinds of VDT jobs for level of stress. A job with rigid work procedures was found to yield higher stress levels for its performers.

Table 2-2
Potential Causes of Work Stress

- Rigid work procedures
- Oversimplified, repetitive and routine jobs
- Lost sense of job meaning
- Lack of control
- Heavy workloads
- Pressures for performance
- Monitored performance
- Disrupted social relationships
- Reduced status and self-esteem
- Reduced mobility
- Concern for safety
- Concern for career and job future

Oversimplified, repetitive, and routine jobs. Oversimplification, repetitiveness and routineness create boredom and monotony. Boredom and monotony were cited in the studies by Smith *et al* (1981) and Stammerjohn *et al* (1981) as among the most important factors in job stress. Oversimplified and repetitive jobs do not permit office personnel to utilize their education and experience, so they lack challenge. It is interesting to compare the activities of office VDT users and video-game players. Both activities require simultaneous viewing of a display screen and performance of complex manual-dexterity tasks. However, the challenge of winning makes the video game interesting and fun, while the lack of challenge in the office job often leads to boredom.

Lost sense of job meaning. One feels little sense of accomplishment if the fruit of one's labors does not yield a tangible product, and one that is demonstrably shaped by human craftsmanship. Many automated jobs are but a small part of a larger process in which the final product is rarely visible. Consequently there can be little identification with, or pride in, the end product. Cohen *et al* (1982) also found a lack of job meaning to be a distinguishing feature of more highly stressful jobs.

Lack of control. Automated systems often do not permit people to exercise control over the manner, order, and pace of their work. Tasks must be performed in the prescribed way, in the prescribed order, and at a pace dictated by the system's response time. The psychological need for autonomy is severely threatened. Cohen *et al* (1982) found lack of autonomy to be another distinguishing feature of highly stressful jobs. A number of researchers have found that being able to exercise control over the work situation can relieve many stressful work situations, as indicated clearly in studies by Gardell 1979, Johansson *et al* 1978, Karasek 1979, Karasek *et al* 1981, and Frankenhaeuser 1979. People simply cannot perform at a steady stream of excellence.

A recent report by the Opinion Research Corporation indicates that job dissatisfaction caused by lack of control is creeping into the ranks of middle management as well. Many managers are finding themselves to be simple passers of information up and down through the corporate hierarchy.

Heavy workloads. Automation frequently brings with it a demand for high production standards or work output quotas. An employee is often asked to perform at maximum rates for long periods of time, which denies him or her peaks and valley of normal performance. When valleys do occur, they usually are imposed by the system through slow response times or down time, rather than being a reflection of human needs.

Pressures for performance. Constant pressures to achieve high performance and to achieve a machine-like efficiency may be both outwardly imposed (by management) or inwardly imposed (by the worker). Pressures for performance were another distinguishing feature of stressful jobs in the study by Cohen *et al* (1982).

Monitored performance. Automated systems can easily be monitored through keystrokes, pages created, or transactions processed. Monitoring conjures up grim images of "Big Brother" for many. A Canadian government-appointed task force regarded close monitoring of work as "...an employment practice based on mistrust and lack of respect for basic human dignity. It is an infringement of the rights of the individual..." (Labour Canada Task Force, 1982). Others argue, however, that the power of monitoring can work for the individual. It provides an objective measure of performance that is hard to dispute. It appears that monitoring itself is not the danger, but whether the worker is informed, and how the results are interpreted and used.

Disrupted social relationships. Automation can seriously impair or destroy the social relationships that exist in the office. People need to encounter and interact with others. Social reinforcement of the peer group is important to many people.

Reduced status and self-esteem. The negative qualities of automation, taken in total, can impair a person's conception of worth and self-esteem. It is important that one have some pride in oneself and a sense of contribution to an ultimate goal.

Reduced mobility. Being tied to a VDT reduces one's mobility. Calmer, more positive feelings are associated with mobility (Johansson 1980).

Concern for safety. A critical concern for safety is being threatened by fears of health hazards associated with using VDTs. (This issue will be addressed later.)

Concern for career and job future. As computers perform more of the tasks accomplished by clerical personnel, employment opportunities will diminish. European studies indicate a 15% to 20% clerical job loss in the next 10 to 20 years. Some experts feel that since many clerical positions are filled by women, and few women are promoted to professional ranks because of a lack of technical knowledge and prevailing management attitudes, job opportunities for women will thereby diminish. Being replaced by a machine is a valid fear expressed by many.

Some Implications

Psychosocial problems and the physical ailments associated with posture and vision cannot be neatly divided into separate categories, nor can the effects of the hardware, the system, the environment, and an organization's management. The worker, too, must be viewed not just as one entity, but as a group of individuals with a variety of needs, interests, attitudes and susceptibilities.

In the past we have tended to look upon the VDT as a collection of steel, plastic, glass, silicon chips and electrons — a physical entity to blame for many of today's perceived ills. We have also looked at the worker as a kind of robot, a standard collection of muscles, bones, and fluids, adaptable to almost anything and immune from feeling, emotions, and damage to the body or psyche. We have looked at the work environment as either a placid lake or as a raging sea serving as a battleground between management and worker, between management and unions. We have looked at the worker as an unnecessary expense, something that can be replaced by a machine with far less cost, both financially and emotionally.

Our vision has tended to be safe and rather narrow. To broaden it is frightening, but broaden it we must. What, then, are the implications of what we know today and what should be the future directions?

The VDT, and the VDT workstation, play a role in reported discomforts. A portion of the reported problems appear to be real. The physiology of the human eye and body is not always compatible with the way VDTs are manufactured and installed. VDTs have been manufactured with display characteristics that can fatigue the human eye, and with components arranged to force their users to assume uncomfortable, constrained, and fatiguing postures. VDTs have also often been installed in offices in a haphazard way with little thought to good viewing and operating conditions.

Use of VDTs need not be physically fatiguing, however, as evidenced by the people and studies that report no problems. A properly designed VDT and good work environment, while probably not totally devoid of discomforts in today's state of the art, can be made much more comfortable to work with than is commonly the case. Solutions to problems, however, cannot be accomplished by independently addressing the equipment and environment. One problem, for example, the large luminance contrast between a dark display screen and the brighter work environment, can be resolved by brightening the display screen or darkening the room. It might even be resolved by redesigning the task so as not to require so many eye movements between the display screen and the surrounding materials.

Job content also plays a significant role in reported discomforts. Reports of physical ailments can be influenced by the content of the job being performed. Some studies (Smith *et al* 1981, and Coe *et al* 1980) have found higher incidences of physical complaints among clerical users than among professional users of VDTs. The job content of the professional users included flexibility in accomplishing goals, control over the tasks, utilization of experience and education, and satisfaction and pride in an end product — the kinds of qualities missing from many clerical tasks.

The impact of the job, and the design of the system, have a much larger impact on satisfaction and work stress than many early researchers suspected. The psychosocial needs can overshadow physical needs in a variety of human experiences. Imagine the strains and discomforts imposed on the body of the marathon runner or the driver of a racing car in Indianapolis in late May. The gratification one receives for these kinds of endeavors is certainly not physical.

Length of working time plays a role in reported discomforts. Johansson and Aronsson (1980) found that as the amount of working time at various VDT jobs increased, so did the percentage of workers expressing psychosocial problems. This study corroborates what has long been assumed. Shorter time periods at VDTs provide opportunities to rest muscles and permit a greater variety in movements and tasks. Studies have yet to be made on optimum time periods, but observation indicates that two hours or less a day at the VDT relieves many of the physical problems.

Individual differences play a role in susceptibility to discomfort. No two people are alike. Human physiques, traits, and sensitivities are distributed along the normal distribution curve. The viewing angle of a VDT located in a standardized position may be proper for one person but not for another. One person may perceive display flicker while a second does not in an identical viewing condition. Even the effect of job-related frustrations on people varies. When confronted with on-the-job obstacles, high-ability persons tend to suffer more (Peters 1983). Solutions must consider individual differences; variable opinions and responses are the norm.

Political issues often muddy the water. Issues of discomfort and stress often become intertwined with difficult labor negotiations or attempts at unionization. Facts are submerged under emotions and political strategies. To admit that a problem does or does not exist may strengthen or weaken one's position, depending upon one's viewpoint. Adversarial relationships seldom yield true and meaningful solutions.

Health Hazards

The proliferation of VDTs in the office has given rise to many concerns over possible adverse health effects associated with their use. Reports of unusually high numbers of miscarriages, birth defects and eye cataracts have created feelings of uneasiness among many VDT users. Among commonly cited examples are children with deformities born to four out of seven VDT operators at a Canadian newspaper and seven miscarriages in 12 pregnancies at a mail order computer center in Texas (*Health and Safety Bulletin,* 1982).

Cases such as these have spurred calls for protective measures on VDT use and even legislation to enforce compliance. While most VDT critics agree that the numbers do not prove anything, they do feel the evidence must warrant concern, and to err should be on the side of safety. Others maintain that these high percentages are simply statistical quirks.

In reaction to these concerns, a number of studies of the radiation emission qualities of VDTs have been performed by a variety of governmental and nongovernmental organizations around the world. Among these are Moss *et al* (1977), Weiss and Petersen (1979), Wolbarsht *et al* (1980), Vetter (1979), Cox (1980), Terrana *et al* (1980), Murray *et al* (1981), United States Bureau of Radiological Health (1981), and the *Environmental Health Directorate* (1983).

The kinds of radiation which are thought to be generated by cathode ray tubes (CRTs) and electronic components of VDTs are x-rays, microwaves, radiofrequency, extremely low frequency, ultraviolet, infrared and visible radiations.

Automation Concerns

X-ray. Whenever fast-moving electrons are slowed down or stopped suddenly by a material, x-rays are produced. When electrons from the cathode strike the fluorescent material on the viewing face of a CRT, visible light is emitted. Ideally, all electrons should be converted to visible light. In practice, however, some electrons are converted to x-rays instead. These x-rays are perceived as a potential source of danger to humans.

Measurements of x-ray emissions over a wide variety of models repeatedly show that none are detectable above the natural background levels. The Bureau of Radiological Health looked at 250 VDTs comprising 150 different models. Emission levels 500,000 times lower than the mandatory standard for VDTs have also failed to be detected. X-rays produced by a CRT are of low energy and not very penetrating. Those x-rays produced are absorbed by the glass face and never reach the outside of the device itself. In fact, the thick glass face on the CRT is actually capable of absorbing x-rays of energies considerably higher than those now produced in the VDT.

Microwave. VDTs have no components that can generate microwave radiation. No microwave radiation has been detected in any of the studies.

Radiofrequency (RF). Radiofrequency radiation in a VDT is caused by the rapid on and off pulsing of the voltage as the image is created on the CRT. In some instances radiofrequency radiation has been found near the surface of the VDT. The level, however, decreases very rapidly with distance from the surface, and at distances of about 8 to 12 inches, radiofrequency is either not detectable or well below harmful levels, including the most stringent exposure standards in the world. The level of radiofrequency radiation that has been detected is of the low frequency kind (up to 150 kiloHertz), and the human body is highly reflective of frequencies below 200 kiloHertz. Therefore only a minimal amount of that which is present is actually absorbed by the body.

Extremely low frequency (ELF). Extremely low frequency emissions, or magnetic field intensities, have been found to be of very low intensity. They are comparable to, or even exceeded by, other common electrical and electronic devices found in the home.

Ultraviolet (UV) and Infrared (IR). Ultraviolet and infrared radiation may also be produced at the fluorescent screen by the bombarding electrons. While most of it is also absorbed by the glass surface on the screen, some ultraviolet radiation has been detected at the viewing screen. Where it has been detected, however, the measured levels have been thousands of times lower than those permitted for continuous occupational exposure.

Visible light. The purpose of a CRT is to produce visible light. The amount produced, however, is really quite low. It is about 200 times lower than the outdoor light level on a cloudy day and about 100 times lower than occupational exposure limits.

Based on the results of other studies, and the findings of their own study, the authors of the *Environmental Health Directorate* report (1983) conclude: "There is no reason for any person, male or female, young or old, pregnant or not, to be concerned about radiation health effects from VDTs." Statements like this, however, will probably not end the controversy. With tragedies from asbestos, thalidomide, dioxin, and the medical use of x-rays earlier this century still in our minds, the feeling that science does not know all the answers may very well persist. What if our standards are too high? What if our measuring instruments are not sensitive enough? What if we are measuring the wrong thing? These are representative questions that might still be asked. We must continue to search for answers that assure everyone that the accelerating use of VDTs is a safe path to follow. At the same time we cannot turn away from a tool with so much promise.

The proper course would seem to be to continue the research needed to establish causes and effects while at the same time assuring that VDTs are used properly within the limits of today's knowledge.

REFERENCES

Cakir, A., D.J. Hart and D.F.M. Stewart, *The VDT Manual*, Darmstadt, Federal Republic of Germany, IFRA, 1979.

Coe, J.B., K. Cuttle, W.C. McClellan, N.J. Warden, and P.J. Turner, *Visual Display Units*, Wellington: New Zealand Department of Health, Report W/1/80, 1980.

Cohen, Barbara G.F., Michael J. Smith, and Lambert W. Stammerjohn, Jr., "Psychosocial Factors Contributing to Job Stress of Clerical VDT Operators," *Office Automation Conference Digest;* San Francisco, CA; April 5-7, 1982.

Computerworld. 1983.

Cox, E.A., "Radiation Emissions from Visual Display Units" and "Health Hazards of VDUs?" *Papers presented at a One-Day Conference, the HUSAT Research Group.* Loughborough University of Technology. December 11, 1980. pp. 25-38.

Crane, P.M., "Effects of Work at Video Display Computer Terminals on Vision, Mood, and Fatigue Symptoms"; Unpublished technical report; 1979.

Dainoff, M.J., A. Happ and P. Crane, "Visual Fatigue and Occupational Stress in VDT Operators." *Human Factors* 23 (4), 1981. pp. 421-438.

DeGroot, J.P., "Eyestrain in Video Terminal Users." *Paper presented at the European Conference of Postal and Telecommunications Administrations Symposium on Ergonomics in PTT-Administrations;* The Hague; September 1981.

Elias, R., F. Cail, H. Christmann, M. Tisserand et F. Horvat., "Conditions de Travail Devant les Ecrans Cathodiques. Organisation des Taches et Astreintes de l'Organisme." *Cahiers et notes documentaires* (INRS) No. 101, 1980. p. 499.

Environmental Health Directorate: *"Investigation of Radiation Emissions from Video Display Terminals,"* Canada, 83-EHD-91, 1983.

Ferguson, D., "An Australian Study of Telegraphists' Cramp." *British Journal of Industrial Medicine,* 28, 1971, pp. 280-285.

Frankenhaeuser, M., "Psychoneuroendocrine Approaches to the Study of Emotion as Related to Stress and Coping." *In H.E. Howe & R.A. Dienstabier (Eds.), Nebraska Symposium on Motivation 1978, 1979,* Lincoln: University of Nebraska Press, pp. 123-161.

Gardell, B., "Tjanstemannens Arbetsmiljoer (Work Environment of White-Collar Workers)," preliminary report of the Research Group for Social Psychology of Work, Department of Psychology, University of Stockholm, 1979, Report No. 24.

Grandjean, E., *"Ergonomics Related to the VDT Workstation,"* Swiss Federal Institute of Technology, Department of Hygiene and Ergonomics, Zurich (undated).

Gunnarsson, E., and I. Söderberg, "Eyestrain Resulting from VDT Work at the Swedish Telecommunications Administration." *National Board of Occupational Safety and Health, Staff Conference Summary;* Stockholm. 1980.

Haider, M., and H. Slezak, "Stresses and Strains on the Eyes Produced by Work with Video Display Screens." *Committee on Automation of the Trade Union of Employees in the Private Sector;* Vienna, 1975.

Haider, M., M. Kundi, and Weisenbock, "Strain of the Worker Related to VDU with Differently Colored Characters." *Paper presented at Ergonomic Aspects of Visual Display Units Workshop;* Milan, Italy; March, 1980.

Health and Safety Bulletin, ACTU-VTHC Occupational Health and Safety Unit. Editors: John Mathews, Nick Calabrese (ISSN 0727-3304), Carlton South, Victoria, Australia. 1982.

Hedman, L., and V. Briem, "Changes in Focusing Accuracy of VDU Operators as a Function of Age, Hours Worked, and Task." *Abstracts: International Scientific Conference on Ergonomic and Health Aspects in Modern Offices;* Turin, Italy; Nov. 7-9, 1983.

Hultgreen, G.V., and B. Knave, "Discomfort Glare and Disturbances from Light Reflections in an Office Landscape with CRT Display Terminals," *Applied Ergonomics,* 5(1), 1974, pp. 2-8.

Hünting, W., E. Grandjean and K. Maeda, "Constrained Postures in Accounting Machine Operators," *Applied Ergonomics,* 11(3), 1980, pp. 143-149.

Johansson, G., "Individual Control in Monotonous Tasks: Effects on Performance, Effort, and Physiological Arousal," *Reports from the Department of Psychology,* University of Stockholm, 1980.

Johannson, G., and G. Aronsson, *Stress Reactions in Computerized Administrative Work,* Stockholm, 1980.

Johansson, G., G. Aronsson, and B. Lindstrom, "Social Psychological and Neuroendocrine Stress Reactions in Highly Mechanized Work," *Ergonomics,* 21, 1978, pp. 583-599.

Karasek, R.A., "Job Demands, Decision Latitude, and Mental Strain: Implications for Job Redesign," *Administrative Science Quarterly,* Vol. 24, 1979. pp. 285-311.

Karasek, R.A., D. Baker, F. Marxer, A. Ahlbom, and T. Theorell, "Job Design Latitude, Job Demands, and Cardiovascular Disease: A Prospective Study of Swedish Men," *American Journal of Public Health.* Vol. 71, 1981. pp. 694-705.

Labour Canada Task Force, "In the Chips: Opportunities People Partnerships." *Report of the Labour Canada Task Force on Micro-Electronics and Employment,* Members: E. Margaret Fulton, Zavis Zeman, Jeannine David McNeil, Murray S. Hardie, Harish C. Jain, Ratna Ray, Cat. No. L35-1982/IE, 1982.

Läubli, Th., W. Hünting and E. Grandjean, "Postural and Visual Loads at VDT Workplaces — Part 2: Lighting Conditions and Visual Impairments," *Ergonomics,* 1982.

Maeda, K., "Occupational Cervicobrachial Disorder and Its Causative

Factors." *Journal Human Ergology* 6. pp. 193-202. 1977.

Meyer, J.J., R. Gramoni, S. Korol et P. Rey, "Quelques Aspects de la Charge Visuelle aux Postes de Travail Impliquant un Ëcran de Visualisation," *Le Travail Humain,* 42, 1979, pp. 275-301.

Moss, C.E., W.E. Murray, W.H. Parr, J. Messite, and G.J. Karches, "A Report on Electromagnetic Radiation Surveys of Video Display Terminals," *National Institute of Occupational Safety and Health Report DHEW (NIOSH),* No. 78-129, Cincinnati, 1977.

Mourant, R.R., R. Lakshmanan, and M. Herman, "Hard Copy and Cathode Ray Tube Visual Performance — Are There Differences?" *Proceedings of the Human Factors Society — 23rd Annual Meeting;* Santa Monica, CA; 1979, pp. 367-368.

Murray, W.E., *et al.,* "Potential Health Hazards of Video Display Terminals," *NIOSH Research Report,* DHHS (NIOSH) Publication No. 81-129, 1981.

Nishiyama, K., T. Uehata, and M. Nakaseko, "Health Aspects of VDT Operators in the Newspaper Industry." *Abstracts: International Scientific Conference on Ergonomic and Health Aspects in Modern Offices;* Turin, Italy; Nov. 7-9, 1983.

Ong, C.M. "Workplace Design and Physical Fatigue: A Case Study in Singapore." *Abstracts: International Scientific Conference on Ergonomic and Health Aspects in Modern Offices;* Turin, Italy; Nov. 7-9, 1983.

Patkin, Michael, Personal Conversation, Whyalla, South Australia, June 14, 1983.

Peters, Lawrence, "Battling the Office Blues," *Office Administration and Automation,* 1983.

Ryburg, J., Personal Conversation, Ann Arbor, MI, November, 1981.

Sauter, S.L., "Predictors of Strain in VDT Users and Traditional Office Workers," *Abstracts: International Scientific Conference on Ergonomic and Health Aspects in Modern Offices;* Turin, Italy; Nov. 7-9, 1983.

Schurick, Jane M., Martin G. Helander, and Patricia A. Billingsley, "Critique of Methods Employed in Human Factors Research on VDTs," *Proceedings of the Human Factors Society — 26th Annual Meeting;* Santa Monica, CA; 1982.

Smith, M.J., B.G.F. Cohen, L.W. Stammerjohn, Jr., and A. Happ, "An Investigation of Health Complaints and Job Stress in Video Display Operations," *Human Factors 23(4),* 1981, pp. 387-400.

Snyder, H.L. and G.B. Taylor, "The Sensitivity of Response Measures of Alphanumeric Legibility to Variations in Dot Matrix Display

Parameters," *Human Factors 21,* 1979, pp. 457-471.

Stammerjohn, L.W., Jr., M.J. Smith, and B.G.F. Cohen, "Evaluation of Workstation Design Factors in VDT Operations," *Human Factors 23(4),* 1981, pp. 401-412.

Starr, Steven J., Claudia R. Thompson and Steven Shute, "Effects of Video Display Terminals on Telephone Operators," *Human Factors 24(6),* 1982, pp. 699-711.

Teniswood, C.F., *Health and Safety Bulletin #12,* ACTU-VTHC Occupational Health and Safety Unit, Carlton South, Victoria, Australia, May, 1982.

Terrana, T., F. Merluzzi, and E. Giudici, "Electromagnetic Radiations Emitted by Visual Display Units," *Ergonomic Aspects of Visual Display Terminals,* (Eds. E. Grandjean and E. Vigliani), Taylor and Francis Ltd. London, 1980, pp. 13-21.

"An Evaluation of Radiation Emission from Video Display Terminals," United States Bureau of Radiological Health, HHS Publication FDA 81-8153, 1981.

Vartebedian, A.C., "Legibility of Symbols on CRT Displays." *Applied Ergonomics,* 1971, pp. 130-132.

Vetter, H., "Health Hazards Associated with the Use of Visual Display Units," *IAEA Report,* 1979.

Weiss, M.M. and R.C. Petersen, "Electromagnetic Radiation Emitted from Video Computer Terminals," *American Industrial Hygiene Association Journal,* 40, 1979, pp. 300-309.

Wodka, Michael A., "Which Light to See?" *Course — Office Automation: The Facility Management Perspective,* Facility Management Institute, Ann Arbor, MI 1982.

Wolbarsht, M.L., F.A. O'Foghludha, D.H. Sliney, A.W. Guy, A.A. Smith, Jr., and G.A. Johnson, "Electromagnetic Emission from Visual Display Units; A Nonhazard," *Ocular Effects of Non-Ionizing Radiation, Proceedings, Society of Photo-Optical Instrumentation Engineers,* Volume 229, 1980.

Chapter Three
WORKSTATIONS

Integration of the physical components of the environment that enable a person to perform a job comfortably, efficiently, accurately, and with a sense of satisfaction begins with the design of the workstation. A workstation may be simple, including only a desk, storage facilities, and a chair. Or it may be complex, incorporating extensive storage facilities, visual display units, large working areas and much more.

Recently the term *executive workstation* has achieved wide usage within the office automation movement. As it is used, however, this term encompasses nothing more than a terminal and its associated software. The true definition of a workstation is much broader than this, since the terminal is but one ingredient.

Workstation Problems Caused by the VDT

The VDT is a large device. It has often been treated like a typewriter, being placed on a convenient desk or table where it will physically fit. Whether this location matches the requirements of the job or the person using it has escaped attention. As a result, many VDT users have been forced to cope with three critical problems: awkward terminal operating positions, lost workspace, and inefficient workspace organization.

Awkward Operating Positions. Problems caused by placing VDTs on standard desks include:
- keyboards too high or low;
- display screen too high or low;
- display screen too near or far away.

Being forced to maintain an awkward operating position has led to the problems associated with the neck, shoulder, arm, and back, as described in the previous chapter.

Springer (1980) describes the results of a survey of insurance company employees which demonstrates the kind of problems that can result from improper work environment design. The company surveyed 384 office personnel 90 days before and after installing a computer-inquiry system. The survey assessed worker attitudes on a variety of work environment factors related to the new system. Sixty-two percent of the respondents reported some physical discomfort while using display terminals with traditional furniture, and 74 percent of those said that back problems were the primary discomfort.

Lack of Workspace. VDTs crowd desktops. Their large size consumes anywhere from 20 to 40 percent of the available work surface. If the amount of paper handled at the newly automated job does not decrease (which is often the case), or if all manual tasks are not eliminated (which is also often the case), a workspace crisis develops. The workers are usually left to solve the problem themselves. The result is a constant layering, shuffling, and losing of important materials. Signs of this condition are:
- materials stored off the desk;
- materials piled on top of the VDT;
- papers taped to the front of the VDT;
- items stacked on other items;
- laps being used to hold manuals or other materials;
- excessive opening and closing of drawers.

Inefficient Workspace Organization. Lack of workspace leads to inefficient workstations. Papers and tools are poorly organized. Desk components are not displayed to best advantage and reshuffling makes it difficult to remember their location. Time-consuming visual searches must be performed. Economy-of-motion problems also occur. Objects are positioned not in the best sequence but wherever space is available. Manual transition times are greatly increased. An analysis of one organization's workstation revealed five different locations for workstation input/output materials and four different locations of storage of manuals.

Such workstation problems rob the system and the worker of effectiveness. The VDT can no longer be viewed simply as an entity in and of itself. It is but one component in a much larger complex.

Workstation Design

Good workstation design depends upon proper construction and arrangement of the job "parts" so that they work well together. Springer (1982) asked office workers what characteristics of workstations were of greatest importance to them. Their answers are summarized in Table 3-1. The most important characteristics were comfort, the ability to adjust furniture themselves, and the ability to adjust the writing surface, terminal screen surface, and keyboard surface.

A workstation is a collection of many ingredients, the shape of which is formed by technology, the task to be performed, and the various human needs. The design structure and process is illustrated in Figure 3-1. Design will always follow a systems approach and be directed toward maximum human effectiveness.

A Shaping Influence: Technology

A workstation will reflect the demands of technology. We are now witnessing a revolution in workstation design brought about by the VDT. Technology has not yet, however, been totally integrated into the workstation. Workstations are still structured around the technology. Technology is still, for the most part, represented by a stand-alone device absorbed into the workstation as best as possible. This is sure to change as terminals become smaller and less expensive. The use of VDTs as display/work surfaces is on the horizon.

Another technology that will have a profound influence on workstation design is voice recognition and talking computers. An electron gun is quiet, a keyswitch almost so. But large numbers of people speaking at, or listening to, their computers will generate acoustical problems that today's office and workstations are poorly prepared to confront. This will be discussed further in subsequent chapters.

A Shaping Influence: Tasks

A workstation also reflects the tasks to be performed. A thorough

Table 3-1
**Workstation Characteristics of
Greatest Importance to Office Workers**

	Average Valence	Rank
General Features		
Comfort	7.0	1
Amount of workspace	6.2	2
Ability to adjust furniture oneself	5.2	3
Amount of storage space	4.3	4
Ease of adjustment	4.3	4
Amount of light available	4.2	6
Privacy	3.3	7
Noise control	2.7	8
Desk Characteristics		
Writing surface height adjustment	8.1	1
Terminal screen height adjustment	7.9	2
Terminal keyboard height adjustment	7.9	2
Separate heights for terminal screen and keyboard	7.9	2
Terminal screen tilt	6.9	5
File drawer storage	6.5	6
Shelves	6.2	7
Terminal keyboard tilt	5.6	8
Terminal viewing distance adjustment	5.6	8
Locking storage area for personal items	5.1	10
Chair Characteristics		
Seat height adjustment	8.9	1
Backrest height adjustment	8.2	2
Ability to swivel while seated	7.8	3
Back tilt adjustment	6.6	4
Arms	5.6	5
Seat tilt adjustment	5.2	6
Ability to lean back	5.2	6
Carpet casters	4.8	8
Footrest	2.8	9

Figure 3-1
Workstation Design

TASKS/JOBS ▼   ▶ TECHNOLOGY

WORKSTATION
- Computer terminals
- Communication devices
- Task-support tools
- Storage facilities
- Work/display surfaces
- Book-support facilities
- Lighting
- Acoustics
- Walls
- Space

▲

HUMAN NEEDS
- Intellectual
- Anthropometric
- Motivational
- Aesthetic
- Social
- Sensory
- Ambient

analysis of the user's tasks must precede design. Designers must clearly define and understand both emergency and routine functions, specific operational requirements (how much, how fast, and how frequent), the sequence of operations, and the information flow necessary to efficiently accomplish the tasks. The product of this analysis should be a set of specifications that describe workstation components and how those components interrelate. If designers fail to perform good task analyses, important components could be forgotten or a poorly integrated collection of parts could be created. The result would be a workstation unsuitable for the human tasks to be performed there.

The Task, the VDT and the Workstation. The per-capita ratio of white-collar workers to display terminals in today's offices is rapidly diminishing. Ratios of 10-to-1 and lower are common in many organizations. By 1990, the estimated nationwide ratio will be about two to three workers to every terminal.

While it is clear that the VDT has not yet been successfully integrated into the workstation, it is also clear that the ultimate solution will be more than one simple set of specifications. The characteristics of the task and frequency of terminal use will yield a series of alternatives.

Until recently, terminal use environments were poorly understood. The relationship between frequency of terminal use, terminal location, the kinds of task done, and human effectiveness may have been in our awareness but had never been fully defined and described. This is rapidly changing as a result of a research effort started by the Facility Management Institute (Ryburg, 1982). By studying a number of large companies, the institute has identified four basic ways that terminals are typically employed in organizations. They have also related these employment profiles to usage characteristics, tasks, and the impact on worker effectiveness.

Regional terminals are groups of terminals in one location which support large groups of mostly professional or technical people. A walking distance of 50 to 100 feet from the workstation to the terminal area is common, as are frequent return trips. One community terminal can support 10 to 20 workers as long as each worker's tasks demand terminal use only about five percent of the time.

Regional terminals are placed in standardized environments with little concern given to varying human needs. Varying requirements for differing amounts of workspace, privacy, screen viewing distance, and body comfort can seldom be fulfilled. Since the users are usually high-salaried professionals, the dollar cost of these inefficiencies can be high.

Satellite terminals consist of terminals placed closer to where people do their work. The processing needs of four to six people may be satisfied by one terminal located just a few feet away from their workstations. Usage characteristics and terminal workstation design deficiencies are similar to those of the regional variety.

Cluster terminals consist of one or more terminals placed in a fixed position within equal reach of two to four people. No one person has optimum access to such a terminal, but all are within seated arm's reach. Cluster use normally evolves when a person's time requirements for using the VDT are in the 10 to 15 percent range. Usage may increase to 20 to 30 percent of each one's time, at which point contention develops for access, and queuing results if four people are sharing. Since clustering results in terminals being placed outside of the primary work zone, optimal use relationships do not exist for anyone. Long and fatiguing reaches to the keyboard may be required and viewing distance and angle may be unsatisfactory.

Dedicated terminals are those placed in a workstation for the use of only one worker. They can be optimally located for this purpose and are normally found when 20 percent or more of a worker's tasks require terminal usage. Dedicated terminals are, of course, the largest and fastest-growing kind of terminal environment. Their impact on the worker has been described in this and the previous chapters.

Given these environments, the different kinds of terminal users (such as senior management, middle management, professional, technical, and clerical), and the different kinds of tasks (decision support, teleconferencing, data entry, etc.), the Facility Management Institute has defined more than 60 different potential workstations that may be needed to support the automated office. The implications of the task will have a great impact on the workstation's structure and the structure of the office itself.

A Shaping Influence: Human Needs

Workstation design must also reflect human needs, including biological (anthropometric, sensory, and ambient) and psychological (intellectual, social, motivational, and aesthetic).

Anthropometric factors refer to body dimensions and physical capabilities, such as seated or standing heights, reach lengths, arm angles in keying, and viewing angles. These greatly affect personal comfort in performing office tasks. The ideal design is one that enables a person to achieve economy of effort. Designs insensitive to anthropometrics cause fatigue, and a fatigued person will make more errors and will not perform tasks as quickly.

Sensory factors involve the characteristics of human senses, such as sight and hearing, which have a decided impact on the effectiveness of design. Designers should consider the directional nature of sight in locating displays, and the limits imposed by legibility and eye convergence requirements in positioning source documents and display screens. Similarly, the nondirectional nature of hearing will influence the location of auditory signals. The design must also try to minimize distractions within the workstation and from external sources.

Ambient factors are the ambient conditions affecting workstation design — light, sound, temperature and humidity. These factors will be discussed in subsequent chapters. Workstation design should not inhibit the establishment of their optimum ranges.

Intellectual factors include the informational requirements needed to support one's memory and information processing capabilities. These may vary among different tasks for one person, or they may vary among different people for the same task. Informational needs may be supported by the system through use of prompts and help facilities, or they may be supported by various hard-copy materials such as procedure manuals, job aids, checklists, or training documents. In either case, the need for informational support must be satisfied by the workstation design.

Social factors refer to the interpersonal relationships (either face-to-face or electronic) that the workstation design must facilitate. Face-to-face requirements may range from conference privacy to direct visual and physical access among members of the same or related work groups. The design must also reflect the workers' interactions with communications devices, such as telephones, visual display units, and teleconferencing facilities.

Motivational factors are important in workstation design since it is now recognized that workstations can have a significant impact on attitudes toward work. A design that permits fulfillment of basic human motivational needs will contribute to effective performance. Some important basic needs identified by behaviorists are *privacy, individuality, status,* and *belonging,* each which is described below.

Workstations

Privacy is the ability to regulate or control social interaction and interruptions. It means being able to engage in conversations that require confidentiality and security, freedom from interruptions to concentrate on creative work, security from the discomfort of people standing nearby, and protection from noise and other distracting sounds. People attempt to maintain privacy by defining the following conditions (Kaplan 1978, Hunsaker 1981):

1. Territoriality: an area with boundaries that is under the control of workers and designed for their exclusive use. When fixed boundaries do not exist, people create a semi-fixed territory by establishing boundaries with such objects as notebooks, coffee cups or jackets over the backs of chairs. While legal right to the territory is not granted, proprietary right is assumed and territory violation may lead to feelings of loss, anger, and a desire to regain the space.
2. Personal space: an immediate space or bubble that is constantly around a worker and is inviolate.
3. Interpersonal space: the distance people regulate between themselves and others. Research has found that adult American business people interact in the following four zones: (a) *intimate zone*, which ranges from actual physical contact to a two-foot distance; (b) *personal zone*, which ranges from about two to four feet; (c) *social zone*, which extends from about four to 12 feet; and (d) *public zone*, which stretches from about 12 feet to the limits of sight and hearing. The importance of these zones is rarely recognized until a violation occurs, when tension and distrust may occur and effective communication may be hindered.
4. Crowding: perception and reaction to the number of people within an area, not as a population density but as a subjective and changing experience.

Privacy does not necessarily mean aloneness; it simply means controlling interpersonal situations by controlling the physical environment. Privacy requirements may change as activities and feelings change.

Individuality is the motivational mechanism by which people control and own their environment. People typically try to put a personal stamp on what is theirs. Something initially strange and hostile then becomes something uniquely theirs with which they are comfortable. Bomberg (1979) provides an interesting paper on this topic.

Status, another motivational factor, involves possession of a workstation that is commensurate with one's title and experience. Status in the office is reflected in greater privacy, preferred locations, and the kinds of objects that comprise the workstation. Hunsaker (1981) provides the following generalizations about status:

Privacy and Location-Related Indicators of Status:
- More personal territory is better than less.
- Private is better than public.
- Higher is better than lower.
- Close to the top executive is better than far away.
- *In* is better than *out*.

Object-Related Indicators of Status:
- Big is better than small.
- Many is better than few.
- Clean is better than dirty.
- Neat is better than messy.
- Expensive is better than cheap.
- Very old or very new is better than recent.
- Personal is better than public or company-issued.

A sense of *belonging* is also important to people. Workstation design should foster identification with or belonging to a group.

Aesthetic factors is the final component of workstation design. The workstation configuration should be pleasing to the eye. But a danger to be avoided and a mistake made innumerable times is placing aesthetic considerations before performance criteria. Any design feature should enhance, or at the very least not hinder, human performance.

Workstation Design Guidelines

A well-designed workstation, then, must reflect the needs of technology, the task to be done, and its human occupant. Its ultimate objective is to foster effective human performance. The following offers a series of design guidelines directed toward achieving a properly structured workstation. First the concept of adjustability is discussed. Then the individual components of the workstation are examined in greater detail.

Adjustability. The postural and visual problems associated with using display terminals are being solved by providing easily adjustable workstation work surfaces, display surfaces, and chairs. Arguments in favor of adjustability are summarized in Table 3-2. The installation of a VDT on a traditional desk of fixed height suggests that:
- Work posture is not important.

Workstations

> **Table 3-2**
> **Reasons for Adjustable Workstations**
>
> - People vary in all dimensions
> - Body proportions vary widely within any group
> - Different tasks may require different work layouts
> - People vary their postures and positions frequently
> - Medical problems, aches, and pains may require temporary changes for comfort
> - Experience may change a person's preference for position
> - Older people may require up to 10 times more light
> - Temperature, humidity, air flow, and angle of sunlight may require position shifts
> - Fatigue may make frequent condition changes desirable
> - Different people may occupy the workstation over short periods of time
> - A feeling of control over the work situation is fostered

- People adapt easily to awkward arrangements.
- All VDT users possess the same seated eye and elbow height.
- Workstation costs are more important than human costs.

The concept of adjustability is now being studied experimentally with positive results. Springer (1982) found a 10 to 15 percent performance improvement for adjustable workstations when compared to conventional workstations. Dainoff *et al* (1982) found a 20 to 25 percent improvement in performance when comparing well and poorly adjusted workstations. The latter also found that a decrease in musculo-skeletal complaints resulted from properly designed workstations. A Louis Harris survey sponsored by the New England Life Insurance Company found that productivity increased by as much as 17 percent when workstations were designed to meet the needs of people using them (Emanuel & Saunders, 1983).

A number of research efforts have also reported means and ranges of setting levels for a variety of adjustable workstation components. A compilation based on the results of studies by Grandjean *et al* (1982), Miller and Suther (1981), and Springer (1982) is described in Table 3-3. The second column *(Low)* indicates the lowest value reported in

Table 3-3
**Preferred Adjustments
of Keyboard, Display, Support Surface and Seat***

	Low	Mean	High
Keyboard			
Support Surface Height	22.0" (M)	24.8" (M)	34.7" (G)
		28.1" (G)	
Home Row Height	25.1" (M)	27.8" (M)	37.8" (G)
		31.2" (G)	
Angle	14° (M)	18° (M)	25° (M)
Display			
Screen Height (Center)	30.8" (M)	36.4" (M)	45.2" (G)
		40.2" (G)	
Support Surface Height	24.0" (S)		32.0" (S)
Distance from Front of Support Surface	19.5" (G)	25.0" (G)	30.8" (G)
Screen Inclination (Degrees Back from Vertical)	-2° (G)	4° (G)	13° (G)
		3° (M)	
Viewing Angle (Degrees Down from Horizontal)	-2° (G)	9° (G)	26° (G)
Viewing Distance	16.0" (S)	20.0" (S)	36.3" (G)
		29.6" (G)	
Seat			
Height	12.6" (M)	16.0" (M)	24.0" (S)
		18.7" (G)	
Sample Standing Height	58" (S)	66" (G)	76" (S)
		67" (M)	

(M) = Miller and Suther (1981)
(S) = Springer (1982)
(G) = Grandjean *et al* (1982)

*Adapted from Grandjean *et al* (1982), Miller and Suther (1981), and Springer (1982) — see references at end of chapter.

Workstations

any of the studies; the third column *(Mean)* provides the mean setting for each study; and the fourth column *(High)* indicates the highest value reported in any of the studies. The wide variety of settings in each of the dimensions is noteworthy. Further comments on the study results are included in the following sections discussing each component.

Adjustable work-surface heights, then, are recommended because, when properly adjusted, they permit a correct working posture for all workers. No compromises are necessary for workers whose size varies greatly from the average (such as footrests for shorter people). Correct work posture does not normally mean a single fixed posture, but a relaxed, natural one that enables a person to assume a number of alternative postures. Correct work posture is variable, not fixed.

Work surfaces. Workstation work surfaces include the desk top, keyboard and keyboard support surface, display-screen support surface, the display-screen image surface, and source document or other material support surfaces. Critical dimensions include heights above the floor, sizes (length and width), viewing distances, and viewing angles.

Work surface heights are based on the premise that when a worker is correctly seated, the upper arm should be nearly vertical and the lower arm nearly horizontal. For tasks requiring heavy manual effort, the surface should be a little lower to get the help of body weight. For fine work a slightly higher surface may be desirable. Work surfaces that require the upper arm to be raised above the relaxed elbow height increase the metabolic costs of work (Tichauer 1967).

Bex (1971) reported on a European survey that found that the most common work surface heights have decreased from about 30 inches in 1958 to about 28½ inches in 1970. Mandal (1982) reports that while desk tops have been getting lower, people have been getting taller (almost four inches over the past century). This divergence in distance between the desktop height and human height leads to increased flexion and loading of the lumbar region of the back as a person is forced to assume a more bent-over position to work. Lower desks, he concludes, are a contributing factor to back problems and have no obvious advantage. He argues for higher tilting chairs and higher sloping work surfaces. He also reports (1983) that for a paper-reading task, the preferred table height is at least one-half of one's body height.

The adjustable range recommended for working surfaces is 23 to 32 inches above the floor. Bex (1971) suggests 23 to 30 inches. The Grandjean *et al* (1982) data suggest a higher upper limit. A 23 to 32-inch range should cover the majority of desk users. For those cases where adjustability is not possible, a fixed height of 28½ or 29 inches above the floor appears to be the most practical.

The size of the work surface is very task dependent. It is obvious that larger work surfaces are needed to compensate for the space consumed by the VDT. Springer (1982) concluded that a minimum working area of 30 by 48 inches was needed for data entry and inquiry tasks. The minimum depth of the work surface should be at least 32 inches to permit proper viewing distances of desk-standing display screens. Optimum work surface configurations are discussed in the following section.

Work surfaces should be thin and should not possess drawers that can hinder one's movement. All corners should be rounded, not sharp.

Work Surfaces

Height:
- Should be independently adjustable within a range of 23-32 inches above the floor.
- If a fixed height is necessary, it should be 28½ or 29 inches above the floor.

Size:
- The work surface should be large enough to allow tasks to be completed in an efficient and effective manner.

Structure:
- It should have a thin top.
- There should be no skirting drawers to obstruct free movement.
- It should have rounded corners.

Keyboard support surfaces. This element should be adjustable within a range of 23 to 32 inches, and should be independent of that for other working surfaces and the display screen support. The keyboard support surface should allow the keyboard to be positioned up to 12 inches from the front of the table top. This will permit placing source documents or forearm/wrist supports in front of the keyboard, if desired. While the distance between the front of the keyboard and the desk edge should not exceed two to four inches, Grandjean *et al*

Workstations

(1982) found a mean distance of over six inches with some measurements exceeding 12 inches. Increased depth will therefore meet a variety of needs.

Grandjean *et al* collected some data on the use of forearm/wrist supports. They found that 80 percent of the people studied rested their forearms and wrists on a support if one was provided. Without one, however, only 50 percent used the desk surface for this purpose. Forearm/wrist supports were judged as comfortable by 80 percent of their subjects and as uncomfortable by only three percent. The desk itself as a resting place was found to be comfortable by 52 percent and uncomfortable by 21 percent.

Keyboard Support Surfaces

Height:
- The height should be independently adjustable within a range of 23 to 32 inches above the floor.

Depth:
- The depth should permit positioning the keyboard up to 12 inches from the front edge of the desk to allow for source documents and forearm wrist supports.

Display screen surfaces. Proper display height is a function of eye position. A person's normal line of sight is about 10 degrees below the horizontal. The primary display area should be within a 30-degree cone, lowered 10 degrees from the horizontal, so a precise display height above desk level is a function of actual viewing distance. The recommended location for the center of the display area (about 10 to 16 inches above the keyboard support surface), then, must also consider viewing distance.

An optimum screen height will permit a person to read the whole screen without neck bending or stooping. Comfortable viewing angles for reading paper materials in a sitting position have been established by Lehmann and Stier (1961). The mean angle is 38 degrees below horizontal, with a significant majority falling within a range of 26 to 50 degrees. Grandjean *et al* (1982) found the mean angle for viewing a VDT screen was nine degrees with a range of minus two degrees to 26 degrees. This smaller angle shown by VDT viewers must be caused primarily by the physical size of the display screen itself and the reflective characteristics of its screen surface.

The normally recommended viewing distance for VDT display screens is about 13 to 24 inches. IBM (1979) recommends a display viewing distance of 20 inches as best for lessening the probability of visual fatigue from eye convergence and accommodation. Eyeglass wearers, however, will find a shorter distance more comfortable. Reading lenses optimize focusing at about 13 inches (Oestberg 1976). Springer (1982) found that the range of viewing distances for a variety of people (with monofocal, bifocal and trifocal glasses, contact lenses, and no eyeglasses) ranged from 16 to 26 inches with means in the 18- to 20-inch range.

Grandjean *et al* (1982), however, found significantly greater viewing distances in their study — about 23 to 36 inches with a mean close to 30 inches. A major contributing factor to this increase was that the VDT users they studied generally assumed more reclined postures than the upright postures of those who had been measured in laboratory settings. As a result their heads were further from the table edge and the display screen. The result of all this research leads one to believe that adjustability of the display screen distance on a horizontal plane is also desirable.

All viewing surfaces should also be located to achieve uniform viewing distances and thus minimize the need to constantly refocus the eye. Since the normal viewing angle of a VDT is a number of degrees downward, to get the display surface perpendicular to one's line of sight normally requires tilting the display screen an equal number of degrees backward from a vertical line. Ideally this inclination should be adjustable to coincide with differing viewing angles. The mean preferred inclination found by Grandjean *et al* (1982) was four degrees and by Miller and Suther (1981) it was three degrees.

As the screen is tilted backward, the chances of picking up reflections from overhead lighting is increased, however. Direct reflections of overhead light can be minimized by tilting the display screen downward several degrees from the normal line of sight. Several degrees of tilt has a minor effect on the angular size of the characters, but may have a significant effect on the glare problem. Those in the Grandjean *et al* and Miller and Suther studies were apparently tilting their display screens slightly forward from line of sight to minimize reflected glare. The screen inclination range found by Grandjean *et al* was from minus two degrees to 13 degrees. The lower the height of the screen the greater the preferred backward inclination. An adjustable screen inclination with a range of minus five degrees to 45

Workstations

degrees would satisfy most all viewing requirements considering room lighting conditions and preferred viewing angles.

A display screen surface which can be rotated several degrees to the left and right would also serve as a means of reducing undesirable reflections.

Display Screen Surface

Height:
- Should be independently adjustable with screen centerline within a range of 10 to 16 inches above keyboard support surface.

Viewing Distance:
- Should be within a range of 13 to 24 inches.

Screen Inclination:
- Should be adjustable within a tilt range of -5° forward to 45° backward from a vertical display screen.

Source documents. Documents and manuscripts being processed should be positioned as close to the keyboard and display screen as possible in order to minimize eye transition movements. Wide separations will slow down keying and writing. They should also be positioned at uniform viewing distances with other display components. Document holders should also be utilized to achieve uniform viewing planes.

Source Documents

Location:
- Should be positioned close to the keyboard and display screen.

Viewing Distance:
- Should provide a viewing distance similar to the display screen (16 to 24 inches).

Viewing Angle:
- Position documents perpendicular to one's line-of-sight.

Chair. A well-designed chair is one of the most important parts of the workstation. It affects posture, circulation, the amount of effort required to maintain a position, and the amount of pressure on the spine. Thinking is also performed best from a seated position.

The German orthopedic surgeon Staffel constructed the forerunner of the modern office chair in 1884. He stressed the importance of lumbar back support and designed a chair which produced a right-angled, upright position. This posture has been uncritically accepted by experts all over the world and forms the basis of correct sitting posture in many references and texts.

In recent years, however, traditional chair posture has been coming under increasing attack. Mandal (1982) argues that the lumbar support carries only about five percent of the body weight as opposed to the seat pan that carries 80 to 95 percent. He further argues that studies of actual workers almost always show them leaning forward with maximal flexion of their backs. Patkin (1983) calls attention to how often people fidget and move about in their chairs, and how constrained postures yield stiff and lame bodies as free blood circulation is impeded. Grandjean *et al* (1982) describe the postures of their VDT users as often being characterized by leaning backwards, extended legs, a forward bending of the head, no support for the lower spine, and lifted arms.

Adjustability in chair dimensions and providing adequate support for a variety of seated postures is a compelling direction if the evidence is to be believed. (Think for a moment how many times you change your seated posture as you read this monograph.) Perhaps the back problems of the world are more easily solved than we had thought. (It is estimated that half the population of the industrialized world suffers from some sort of back complaint.)

Seat Pan. A correctly adjusted seat height allows the feet to rest comfortably on the floor without pressure on the undersides of the legs above the knees. The knees should be bent at a 90 to 100 degree angle, with 80 to 150 degree angles permissible. The arm, when bent, should form a right angle at the elbow when the hand is resting on the keyboard (or desktop). The seat height should be easy to adjust.

Mandal (1983) found preferred heights to be at least one-third of a person's body height for a page-reading task. One modern way to accomplish this is a gas-action mechanism controlled by a lever under the seat pan. The older kind of adjustment where the seat has to be screwed up or down on its base is tedious and many people just will not use it.

The overall size of the seat pan should be no more than necessary to support a person comfortably. It should conform to the shape of the human buttocks and have a rounded edge at the front to prevent constriction of muscles and blood vessels of the thigh. There must be one-inch clearance from the front edge of the pan to the lower leg or calf.

It is often recommended that the seat slope backward between four and eight degrees but some experts claim this causes or increases backaches. Mandal (1982) argues for a forward slope to straighten out the lumbar curve as in standing. A forward slope brings into play the forces of gravity, however, causing a person to slide forward. The best answer may be an adjustable slope mechanism.

Too hard a seat is uncomfortable, while too soft a seat will not relieve pressures with changes in position. Patkin (1983) makes a "firm" recommendation that the seat should sink in about two inches under average body weight. The seat pan should also be able to rotate 360 degrees without changing height.

Backrest. It is important that the back have support. This support should fit into the small of the back, be padded, and be adjustable, both fore and aft and up and down. A correctly adjusted backrest is positioned at the back of the waist, about one inch higher than the top of the hip bone. High backrests are also desirable as they provide support to the upper back muscles and muscles along the spine. High backrests also enable the body to assume a variety of good resting positions.

Armrest. Armrests provide needed support for the arm from the elbow to the center of the forearm. They should be broad (about four inches), well padded, but not long enough to bump against the desk when sitting up close.

Base. The chair should have five legs for stability and casters or wheels for ease of motion. Wheels enable a person to move about from one part of the desk to another, providing both physical and psychological freedom. They must be well built, however, or they will be an irritation.

Chair

Seat Pan:
- Should be easily adjustable within range of 14 to 24 inches above the floor.
- Size should be approximately 16 by 16 inches.
- Should be parallel to the floor.
- Should conform to the shape of the buttocks.
- Seat edge should be rounded edge at the front.

- Should be neither too firm nor too soft (with about a two-inch sink).
- Should be able to rotate 360° without changing its height.

Backrest:
- Should support the back of the waist.
- Should be easily adjustable in height and angle.
- Should conform to the shape of the lumbar (lower back) region.

Armrest:
- Should be large enough to support a resting elbow in different positions but small enough to not interfere with pulling the chair up close to the work surface.

Base:
- Should have five legs for stability.
- Should be on casters for ease of motion.

Desktop logistics. A well-organized workstation will minimize stretching, aid memorization of component locations and minimize transition distances between various elements. Stretching results in a greater reach but increases muscle loads, which can be fatiguing. Memorization of element locations will make them easy to find without a lot of searching. Minimizing transition distances allows economy of motion and results in more efficient performance.

Hierarchical positioning. The overall configuration of each workstation should be based on a task analysis, and final positioning of components depends on the frequency, sequence, and duration of tasks. A basic rule is that the most frequently used components of the workstation be located within a person's convenient reach, with the elbow resting on the desktop. Writing, reading, and keying tasks will normally occur in this zone, called the primary zone. Elements not frequently used, such as in and out baskets and equipment only occasionally used or waiting to be used, should be located in the secondary zone of the workstation. This zone normally encompasses the area of extended arms' reach. The remaining workstation elements, such as materials and manuals, may be positioned outside of these zones.

Effective use should be made of vertical space. An analysis of several kinds of workstations in a financial organization found that proper organization of workstation elements could reduce transition distances by about 50 percent, and increase productivity by an estimated four to seven percent (Ryburg 1981).

Standardized Locations. Standardized locations of elements will

Workstations

aid memorizing where they are located in the work area. Thus they will be accessed more quickly as visual searches are reduced.

Visual Access. Workstation elements should be displayed to good advantage. Where memorization of exact locations is not possible, a visual search must be able to locate them quickly. Opening and closing drawers greatly contributes to wasted time, as does shuffling through piles of materials. Elements being searched for should be identified clearly and simply. This includes manuals, job aids, forms and keyboard keys. The necessity of using drawers or files to complete processing tasks should be eliminated or minimized. The size of storage units should be appropriate to the size of their contents. The dimensions of the storage unit should not impinge on the workspace needed for manual tasks.

Desktop Logistics

Hierarchical Positioning:
- Position workstation components hierarchically, based upon frequency, sequence and duration of use:
  a. For writing, keying, and reading, use the primary zone, which is the front area of the workspace within bent arms' reach.
  b. For supporting materials and equipment only occasionally used or waiting to be used, use the secondary zone, which is the area of extended arms reach.
  c. For storage purposes, use the remainder of the workspace.
- Provide uniform viewing distances for frequently viewed material.

Standardized Locations:
- Provide standardized locations for workstation elements.

Visual Access:
- Provide visual access to all frequently used workstation elements.

VDTs. Since VDTs are not truly integrated into workstations in the sense that they are generally not built into it, proper integration requires that they be considered as one of the elements in desktop logistics. Location flexibility is a prime consideration. Therefore, only use display terminals that have detachable keyboards. In addition to the differing height-adjustment advantages, the keyboard may be positioned to reflect different tasks and various individual preferences. Large-volume data-entry tasks will require the keyboard to be positioned directly in front of a person, while manual activities with occasional dialogs might find the keyboard better positioned to the side. Either right- or left-handed preferences may be supported equally as well. Detachable keyboards also permit flexibility in positioning source materials in relation to the keyboard and display screen as eye movements are minimized.

Providing for lateral movement of the VDT across the working surface by placing it on wheels or casters permits proper location based on the needs of the task. Forward and backward positioning enables a person to control viewing distances.

VDTs
- Only use VDTs with detachable keyboards.
- Permit source documents and materials to be located:
  a. between the person and the keyboard;
  b. to either side of the keyboard;
  c. between the keyboard and the display screen.
- Provide for moving of the VDT across the working surface:
  a. forward and backward;
  b. laterally.

Configuration. Springer (1982) solicited preferences for a variety of workstation arrangements incorporating VDTs. He found that the most preferred was an L-shaped configuration, one arm possessing the writing surface and the other containing the terminal. An arrangement like this will keep arm reaches to a minimum and maximize the amount of available workspace in the major work zones.

Walls. Robert Propst of Herman Miller Inc., designer of the "Action Office," recommends a three-sided enclosure as the best approach to designing workstation walls. Propst feels this is best because it provides good definition of territory and allows both privacy and the ability to participate. A four-sided enclosure he feels, is "...bad for the wide-awake, activity-oriented person who is isolated, insulated, and remote." Another advantage of enclosures is that they give workers the opportunity to personalize their work spaces. Other writers have suggested that a two-sided enclosure may be satisfactory if the layout of the stations minimizes eye contact and other visual and sound distractions. Such distractions are discussed more fully shortly.

Size. In general, the greater the space between workstations, the more privacy a person will have. These guidelines assume, however, that a noise-control program is in effect in the work area. Without such a program, 3,000 square feet per workstation might not guarantee privacy. Under good acoustical conditions, an area smaller than 200 square feet may be quite satisfactory.

Configuration

Arrangement:
- Provide an L-shaped workstation arrangement that enhances efficiency of motion between the two sections.

Walls:
- Provide a minimum of three walls or sides, with a slightly widened opening.

Size:
- For normal privacy, allow at least 80 square feet per workstation.
- For confidential privacy, allow a minimum of 200 square feet per workstation.

Visual and acoustic distraction control. Acoustic control is accomplished at the workstation by using sound-absorbing materials on the workstation walls. Acoustic and distraction control is accomplished by orienting workstations so that they do not face other people and opening them into zones where little movement occurs.

Visual and Acoustic Distraction Control

- Use workstation walls to block sound transmission and to prevent visual distractions. Walls should be at least five feet high, and preferably six feet high.
- Position workstations so that people are not facing other people.
- Have workstations open to zones where there is little movement.

The office furniture industry has recognized present furniture shortcomings and is moving toward a system approach to workstation design. Task/ambient lighting, component furniture systems, modular storage, and easily-adjustable component heights illustrate this approach. The dramatic increase in the variety of considerations and services that support a VDT (such as lighting, telephone and data communication cables) will in the future make workstations more built-in and fixed in location.

The next major restructuring of the workstation will occur as the components of the computer interface system are included within the working surfaces themselves. Terminals will cease to be instruments supported by a surface, but will become part of the work surface. In some ways the workstation may become one large terminal.

Another technology on the horizon will soon have a large impact on workstation design — talking computers. Voice communications between people and systems will usher in a whole new era of acoustical concerns and solutions as the office din increases while workstation size decreases as a result of more costly office space. The creative worker, while being freed from the mechanics of interfacing with a keyboard, will be exposed to the distractions caused by an escalating major noise source in the office, the human voice.

Ultimately, an effective workstation design is going to require even closer cooperation among all involved parties — furniture manufacturers, terminal manufacturers, facility managers, and computer users. Those who are not yet talking to each other had better start quickly.

REFERENCES

Bex, F.H.A., "Desk Heights," *Applied Ergonomics*, 2, No. 3, 1971, pp. 138-140.

Bomberg, H., "Workflow/Workspace, People vs. the Process: The Case for Personal Space," *Impact: Information Technology*, Jan., 1979.

Dainoff, Marvin J., Laurie Fraser, and B.J. Taylor, "Visual, Musculoskeletal, and Performance Differences Between Good and Poor VDT Workstations: Preliminary Findings," *Proceedings of the Human Factors Society 26th Annual Meeting,* 1982, Santa Monica, CA.

Emanuel, Harold M. and S. Saunders, "Plugging Into the Open Office," *Today's Office,* June, 1983, pp. 29-31.

Grandjean, E., W. Hunting and M. Piderman, "A Field Study of Preferred Settings on an Adjustable VDT Workstation and Their Effects on Body Postures and Subjective Feelings," Department of Hygiene and Ergonomics of the Swiss Federal Institute of Technology, Zurich, June 22, 1982.

Hunsaker, Phillip L., "Proxemics Set Guidelines for Territoriality in Planning Office Spaces," *Contract,* March, 1981.

IBM, "Human Factors of Workstations With Display Terminals," San

Jose, CA, Sept. 1979, G320-6102-1.

Kaplan, A., "Ergonomics of Open Planning Workstations," *Modern Office Procedures,* April, 1978.

Lehman, G. and F. Stier, "Mensch and Gerät," *Handbuch der Gesamten Arbeitsmedizin,* Band 1, Urbana and Schwarzenberg, Berlin, 1961, pp. 718-788.

Mandal, A.C., "The Seated Man — Theories and Realities," *Proceedings of the Human Factors Society 26th Annual Meeting,* 1982, Santa Monica, CA.

Mandal, A.C., "What is the Correct Height of Furniture?" *Abstracts: International Scientific Conference on Ergonomic and Health Aspects in Modern Offices,* Turin, Italy, November 7-9, 1983.

Miller, I. and T.W. Suther, "Preferred Height and Angle Settings of CRT and Keyboard for a Display Station Input Task," *Proceedings of the Human Factors Society 25th Annual Meeting,* 1981, Santa Monica, CA.

Oestberg, O., "Office Computerization in Sweden: Worker Participation, Workplace Considerations and the Reduction of Visual Strain," *Paper presented at the NATO Advanced Study Institute on Man-Computer Interaction,* Mati, Greece, Sept., 1976.

Patkin, Michael, *Problems of Body Dimensions and Eyesight in the V.D.U. Workplace,* Ergon House Publishing, Ltd., Whyalla, South Australia, 1983.

Rough Notes, Aug. 1978. "Weighing the Pros and Cons of Open Plan Office Layout."

Ryburg, Jon, Personal Conversation, Ann Arbor, MI, December, 1981.

Ryburg, Jon, "The Facility Management Implications of Office Automation," *Proceedings — Office Automation Conference,* AFIPS, San Francisco, CA, April, 1982.

Springer, T.J., "Visual Display Units in the Office Environment: Blessings or Curses?" *Paper presented at Human Factors in Industrial Design in Consumer Products,* Tufts University, May 28-30, 1980.

Springer, T.J., "VDT Workstations: A Comparative Evaluation of Alternatives," *Applied Ergonomics,* 13(3), 1982, pp. 211-212.

Tichauer, E.R., "Industrial Engineering in the Rehabilitation of the Handicapped," *Proceedings of the 18th Annual Institute Conference and Convention,* American Institute of Industrial Engr., May, 1967, pp. 171-177.

Chapter Four
LIGHTING

A vital component of any office environment is lighting. Poor or improper lighting can cause eyestrain or headaches, while good lighting can increase a person's productivity. In recent years, as office environments have moved toward open landscapes and specially designed workstations, and as concern has grown over office energy consumption, office lighting has become a highly technical and somewhat controversial topic. Many divergent opinions have been expressed on the quantity, quality, and type of lighting needed to perform tasks efficiently in today's office.

Basically, good lighting is that which fulfills the needs of the worker and causes minimal glare. However, these rather broad statements have multiple implications.

Illumination Levels

Ambient light levels in general office work areas have steadily increased since the introduction of electric lighting. Today, lighting levels in many modern office buildings are in the 90-to-150 foot-candle range. High levels of illumination are preferable for paper-based operations because, generally speaking, more light results in easier reading of paper documents. For example, a life insurance company found that substituting 100 foot-candle lighting for 50 foot-candle lighting improved productivity by 2.8 percent, and productivity improved by 8.1 percent using 150 foot-candles. In an office of 100 workers, improvements in worker accuracy resulted in savings of $17,000 using 100 foot-candles and $52,000 using 150 foot-candles (*Fortune*, 1979). As a consequence, many offices are generally over-illuminated. Areas where reading of documents is not important bathe in light supplied for that purpose.

Office illumination and VDTs, however, have an adversary relationship. Higher levels of lighting make it more difficult to read the VDT by reducing the contrast of its luminous characters with the display background. The whole concept of office illumination, therefore, is being restructured to confront the problems imposed by the VDT. Illumination level is becoming a more technical and complicated consideration as new technologies emerge.

The following general statements can be made about illumination levels:

- In terms of light direction, the central part of one's field of vision should receive the most light, for both attention-getting and physiological reasons. The eyes have a distinct tendency to turn toward light.
- Once one reaches the age of 40, the amount of illumination needed for seeing increases. For people of age 50, 50 percent more light is needed than was required when they were young; for those over 60, 100 percent more light is needed.
- The level of illumination should correspond with the needs of the task being performed.

Glare

Another critical factor in office lighting is the amount of glare it causes one to perceive. Glare results when the level of brightness in one's field of vision is greater than that to which the eye is adapted, thereby causing annoyance. Smaller amounts of glare reduce the ability to discern objects while a great amount of glare may completely block sight. To be considered good, lighting must be free of glare. Since glare increases faster than the illumination level (doubling illumination at least triples the risk of glare), some glare cannot be avoided at high illumination levels.

The most important factor in reducing glare is providing well-balanced luminance contrast between adjacent work areas. Low luminance contrasts cause difficulty in distinguishing fine details, but

Lighting

sharp contrasts can themselves cause glare. To reduce glare, a luminance/contrast ratio of three-to-one between adjacent workstation surfaces is desirable. Positioning light sources so that they are not directly visible and so that light does not reflect directly into the eyes can also reduce glare.

Natural Light

A vital ingredient of the earth's life-support system is light from the sun, or full-spectrum light. For years, people have substituted artificial light for sunlight when the sun is blocked or of insufficient intensity. Recently, photobiologists (those who study light's effects on living creatures) have determined that the wrong kind of artificial lighting can increase fatigue and stress and impair human visual acuity. Often, the consequence is lower worker productivity.

The light that scientists consider proper is full-spectrum sunlight or light from specially designed fluorescent bulbs that closely simulate sunlight. Incandescent bulbs and most fluorescent bulbs are a less-than-optimum light source since they do not produce full-spectrum light. Yet they are commonly used in today's offices.

At Cornell University, students working in a class with full-spectrum fluorescent light experienced a significant increase in visual acuity and less overall fatigue, compared to performance under regular fluorescent light. Russian scientific reports show that full-spectrum lighting in schools helps academic performance, improves student behavior, and lessens fatigue. And in Russian industry it has been demonstrated that, with full-spectrum light, production goes up and absenteeism drops. As a result, many Russian workplaces have mandated this kind of lighting (McCormack 1980).

It has also been found that people favor work environments with windows. Workers frequently indicate that they think daylight is better for eyes than artificial light, and they markedly overestimate the amount of daylight present at their workstations (Wells 1965).

Full-spectrum light can also lessen depression. Scientists at the National Institute of Mental Health report that exposure to this kind of light during the predawn and after-dusk hours effectively lengthens the period of daylight and dramatically buoys a person's mood (Morton 1982).

Light is rated to determine its spectral qualities by the color rendering index (CRI). Natural outdoor light has a CRI of 100, while the

CRI of full-spectrum, fluorescent light is 91. The CRI of standard cool-white fluorescent light is 68, and other fluorescents are 56. This is a relatively new field of illumination, and further understanding of lighting needs and effects is expected in the future.

The following offers guidelines for improving the viewing environment of VDTs, as summarized in Table 4-1.

Visual Display Terminals and Illumination

The illumination characteristics of the environment in which a VDT is used can never be considered independently of the characteristics of the device itself and the task being performed. Hardware considerations, such as the brightness of the display screen, the use of

---

Table 4-1
Visual Display Terminals and Illumination

Maintain proper luminance-contrast ratios in the field of vision
- 1:3 for near field.
- 1:5 for far field.

Minimize direct and reflected glare
- Position light sources outside of the direct line of sight or screen off those in the direct line of sight.
- Position light sources so that their emitted light is not reflected from the screen back toward one's eyes. Use many small light sources instead of a few large ones, or use indirect lighting, or diffused lighting.
- Position lights away from work surfaces.
- Minimize reflectance levels of surrounding room and furniture surfaces. Recommended reflectances are: floors: 20-40%; furniture: 25-45%; business machines: 25-45%; desktops: 25-45%; walls: 40-60%; window blinds: 40-60%; and ceilings: 80-90%.

- Position VDTs so that the display screen is perpendicular to windows.
  a. Provide window blinds that are horizontal, adjustable, full-length, and off-white or grey in color.
  b. Surround windows with a light-colored surface.
  c. Set windows a good distance above the floor.
  d. Construct outdoor window overhangs.

glare-reducing filters, and rotatable and tiltable displays, also play an integral role in solutions to illumination questions. So do such job characteristics as whether a person will be using a VDT exclusively or part time, whether or not paper-based materials must be read, and so forth. Environmental solutions should also not be considered solutions to problems caused by poor system design. Situations that force a person to look many thousands of times a day between the display screen and source materials are better addressed by improving the system. Lighting solutions will only alleviate a symptom, not address a cause.

Maintain proper luminance-contrast ratios. The luminance-contrast ratio is the difference in brightness of the light emitted from different surfaces. Large contrasts in brightness can cause the eye to adapt to the brighter light and pose difficulties in seeing objects that have a much lower luminance. VDTs containing dark display screens and used in bright offices are susceptible to this problem. Sharp contrasts can also cause glare. For best viewing, luminance-contrast ratios in the work area should not exceed one to three between the focus of the visual task and immediately adjacent seeing areas (near field), and one to five for the visual tasks and objects in the peripheral field of vision (far field).

In a recently-reported study, Kokoscha and Haubner (1983) found that work performance is also affected by large luminance differences in the visual field. They feel that the one-to-three contrast ratio requirement may be too restrictive, however.

The proper brightness of a room's light in terms of foot-candles cannot really be specified without considering luminance-contrast ratios. From a practical standpoint, however, the typical VDT used in today's office would probably find light levels in the 45 to 65 foot-candle range satisfactory for jobs requiring both VDT and paper reading. For jobs involving VDT reading only, 10 to 15 foot-candles would be appropriate. Ways of reducing background luminances, in addition to altering the office lighting, include such measures as changing the terminal's location and repainting the walls. These and other factors are described in the following.

Position light sources outside of the direct line of sight. A VDT should never be positioned so that while it is in use a light source is in the user's line of sight. Eliminate the light source or reposition the VDT so that the light is above and slightly in front of the user. If neither of these is possible, screen off the offending light source through the use of a shield, hood, or visor.

Position light sources so that their emitted light is not reflected from the screen back toward one's eyes. Overhead fluorescent lights common in many offices often appear as white bars reflected on the screen's face. These reflections are frequently responsible for the perception of glare. Desk lights at adjacent workstations may also be offenders. When locating VDTs in the office, the positions of existing lights, and their potential for creating reflections and glare, must be considered. Ideally, the plane of the display screen surface should be perpendicular to all visible light sources.

Use many small light sources instead of a few larger ones, or use indirect lighting or diffused lighting. Bright artificial light sources can be subdued by using a variety of techniques, such as by diffusing emitted light from standard ceiling-mounted fixtures, by replacing ceiling fixtures with workstation-mounted ambient light, and by providing task lighting either mounted on the ceiling or directly on the workstation. Advantages and disadvantages of these different approaches will be discussed shortly.

Position lights away from work surfaces. Lights positioned close to work surfaces are another potential source of glare.

Minimize reflectance levels of surrounding room and furniture surfaces. In addition to artificial and natural light sources, a host of other factors may contribute to glare. These include shiny workstation walls, pieces of paper or photos attached to workstation walls, and a white shirt or blouse worn by the VDT user. Anything that causes a contrast in the terminal's viewing surface must be considered a potential source of glare. To minimize these potentials for glare, the reflectance levels of surfaces of walls and objects in the work area and office should not exceed 20 to 50 percent for horizontal surfaces, 40 to 60 percent for vertical surfaces, and 80 to 90 percent for ceilings. Some typical reflectance values for common office wall colors are illustrated in Table 4-2. Bright objects such as wall graphics and pinups should also be carefully positioned so that no disturbing reflections are created.

Position VDTs so that the display screen is perpendicular to windows. To avoid window glare, position the display screen surface perpendicular to windows so that the light strikes the working surface at a right angle. For particularly bright windows it may also be necessary to place a panel between the terminal operator and the window.

Provide window blinds that are horizontal, adjustable, full-length

Lighting

and off-white or grey in color. The amount of light entering a room may be controlled through the use of window blinds. Horizontal, adjustable, full-length blinds permit easy adjustability to compensate for differing conditions of outside brightness caused by the sun's position and clouds. An off-white or grey color minimizes the likelihood of the blind becoming a source of reflection and glare.

Surround windows with a light-colored surface. A light-colored surface surrounding the windows will minimize the luminance-contrast ratio between the window itself and the wall.

Set windows a good distance above the floor. Buildings with an architectural design that permits locating windows well above the floor will eliminate some of the problems caused by waist-high or lower windows. Other remedial measures may still be necessary, however.

Construct outdoor window overhangs. Bright outdoor light can be reduced by providing outdoor window overhangs. Again, further remedial measures may still have to be taken.

The above glare-reduction guidelines are found in McCormick (1976), the *Illuminating Engineering Society (IES) Lighting Handbook* (1972), and a number of other sources. In addition, the IES has adopted a standard procedure for computing the *discomfort glare rating* (DGR) for luminaries and interior lighting (Illuminating Engineering Society 1966). The calculation of DGR ratings for a specific

Table 4-2
Representative Color Reflectance Values

Color Name	Description	Reflectance Percent
Eggshell	White	85
Neutral	Off-White	60
Buttercup	Bright Yellow	52
Mushroom	Light Tan	44
Pumpkin	Medium Orange	31
Apple	Medium Red	16
Sky	Light Blue	14
Wine	Dark Red	4
Eggplant	Purplish-Black	3

lighting layout takes into account most of the factors that affect visual comfort. A derived DGR can then be converted into a *visual comfort probability* (VCP) for any situation. The scheme for estimating a DGR is complex and beyond the scope of this monograph. The IES handbook gives a full description.

Task/Ambient Lighting

The ceiling-mounted fluorescent lighting fixtures commonly found in today's offices contain standard refractors which present to the VDT display screen a very bright surface. These bright surfaces are a primary source of the reflections and glare seen by VDT users. Furthermore, studies have shown that only 20 percent of traditional overhead lighting is directed toward work surfaces. The remaining 80 percent is devoted to lighting for occasional conferences and circulation of people. Since vision is improved when light is directed toward the primary work area, it makes sense to direct more light toward this area, where it is most needed. These factors of increased visual comfort and improved economy have created an interest in task/ambient lighting as a viable concept in the automated office.

Task lighting. Task lighting provides light only where it is needed. It is accomplished by directing light from ceiling sources toward the workstation, building light sources into the workstation, or providing free-standing or attachable desktop lamps. Task lighting at the workstation consists of fluorescent or high-intensity unidirectional lamps directed at the work surface from a position below seated eye level. Task light of this kind, while achieving the aim of directing light where it is needed, has been known to cause the following problems (*Canadian Office* 1978, Brandston 1978):

- Produces bright pools of light that cause eyestrain for individuals who alternate between light and dark areas.
- Produces direct or reflected glare if task lighting is positioned too close to work surfaces.
- Causes eye irritation due to the 60-cycle blink of fluorescent task lamps. (Overhead fluorescent lamps flicker, too, although not as noticeably as from a distance.)
- Causes fluorescing (glow effects) of papers and office materials under halide lamps.
- Produces general discomfort for some people in spaces using stroboscopic (noncontinuous) illumination.

Lighting

The typical under-cabinet-mounted fluorescent task light is often not acceptable for VDTs positioned on the work surface because the light is too far behind the keyboard, and annoying hot spots are generated on the terminal enclosure. There is the added disadvantage of ceiling lights having to be redesigned whenever office layouts change.

In general, it appears that permanently affixed workstation task lighting is more appropriately located to the left or right side of the VDT work surface. Flexible positioned task lighting is the best choice, since the light can be moved to meet changing needs. The traditional architect's arm lamp illustrates this kind of flexibility (although sometimes the arm may get in the way).

Task lighting should possess the following general qualities:
- The light level should be continuously variable and adjustable by the workstation user. The amount of light can then be matched to the exact needs of each person.
- The position of the light should be flexible on both horizontal and vertical planes. The light can then be exactly matched to the task being performed.
- The illumination pattern should be rectangular or elliptical rather than round. Most documents are rectangular in shape.
- Desk space needed for manual activities should not be taken up by the task light.

The greatest problem with task lighting comes from its complexity. It must be developed in conjunction with many factors, such as the size and location of the work surface; the size, location and color of adjacent walls, ceilings and desk surfaces; and a person's work positions. Light sources located closer to these variables will be more influenced by their design. Subtle design changes may cause enormous lighting changes and problems. Some problems have apparently been created by well-meaning workstation designers who did not understand the complexity of the subject.

The importance of task lighting is that it possesses significant advantages if applied properly and under the right circumstances. However, achieving its benefits requires the help of a lighting professional.

Ambient Lighting. Ambient lighting is the general level of illumination provided in the office or work area. When combined with task lighting, ambient lighting should achieve an overall low-level lighting environment punctuated by brighter task lighting where needed. It is felt that this approach is aesthetically pleasing, more economical, and more truly satisfies the visual needs of office workers. Ambient lighting may be provided by lights directed upward toward the ceiling or by the ceiling fixtures themselves.

Upward-directed ambient lighting is affixed to furnishings or pillars above standing eye height and pointed toward the ceiling. It then bounces off the ceiling as indirect light and provides a diffused, low-level, general illumination. For low ceiling (eight to 10 feet) fluorescent lights are satisfactory. For higher ceilings, mercury vapor, metal halide or high-pressure sodium vapor lamps may be necessary.

The advantages and disadvantages of upward-directed and ceiling-mounted lighting schemes are summarized in Table 4-3. Nuckolls (1981) reports studies that indicate this kind of ambient lighting is not energy efficient because of light loss occurring when the light travels upward, is partially absorbed by the 80-percent reflective ceiling, and then travels downward again. Ceiling-mounted lighting has only the direct path to travel.

Ceiling-mounted ambient lighting presents alternatives to the bright standard refractors on ceiling lights, including parabolic louvers of varying sizes, low-brightness lenses and polarizing lenses, as described in the following.

Small-cell parabolic louvers or half-inch parabolic reflectors can be placed between the lamp and the room to reduce the angle of light spread by about 95 percent. Diffuser lenses can be positioned between the lamps and the parabolic reflectors to reduce glare from overhead lights, particularly for workstations located directly beneath the light. Advantages and disadvantages to this design are summarized in Table 4-3. While achieving low brightness, these louvers age poorly, are difficult to maintain, and are not very efficient. Dust and cigarette smoke may build up and affect their brightness and quality, and cleaning is difficult. Light output may drop by 25 to 40 percent. Efficiency is in the 50 to 60 percent range.

Large-cell parabolic louvers may have cell openings as large as 11 inches square and eight inches deep. Light brightness is greater than for the small-cell louver, but maintenance is easier and efficiency is improved. Light output will drop only about 15 percent and efficiency may approach 80 percent.

Low-brightness lenses, though not as dark as the small parabolic louver or as efficient as the large parabolic louver, provide a solid enclosure with comparatively low brightness. Since they require a recessing depth of only five inches they may be useful where recessing depth is restricted.

Lighting

Table 4-3
Advantages and Disadvantages of Various Kinds of Ambient Lighting*

UPWARD-DIRECTED LIGHTING

Advantages
- Moves with furniture and should be in proper position

Disadvantages
- Some component may still end up within the terminal's offending zone, appearing as a light hazy reflection
- Not energy efficient

CEILING-MOUNTED LIGHTING

Small-cell (half-inch) parabolic louvers

Advantages
- Low brightness

Disadvantages
- Ages poorly
- Difficult to maintain
- Not efficient

LARGE-CELL PARABOLIC LOUVERS

Advantages
- More efficient
- Easier to maintain

Disadvantages
- Lamp image visible from directly beneath
- Brighter than small-cell parabolic louvers
- Greater recessing depth necessary

LOW-BRIGHTNESS LENSES

Advantages
- Easier to maintain
- Shallower recessing depth necessary

Disadvantages
- Fewer suppliers
- Not efficient

POLARIZING LENSES

Advantages
- Reduces glare

Disadvantages
- Uneven brightness
- Few suppliers
- Costly

* Adapted from Nuckolls, 1981.

Polarizing lenses produce results similar to those seen when looking through polarized dark glasses.

In sum, task/ambient lighting can help solve office lighting problems posed by VDTs. Extreme care must be taken, however, to provide a quality solution. It is important to avoid shadows as well as bright and dim spots, poorly directed light, and other lighting deficiencies.

Attention to the lighting needs of workers in office systems is now extremely important due to the impact it can have on worker productivity and health. The increasing complexity of office lighting also requires greater involvement of lighting consultants, since proceeding in ignorance may cause more harm than good. More detailed discussions of general lighting and task/ambient lighting may be found in Shellko and Williams (1976), Brandston (1978), LeFort (1978), Shemitz (1978), Marquard (1977), *Canadian Office* (1978), and Nuckolls (1981).

REFERENCES

Brandston, H., "Furniture-Integrated Task/Ambient Lighting," Interior Design, Feb. 1978.

Canadian Office, "New Concepts in Lighting Offer Big Energy Savings," March, 1978.

Fortune, "Productivity and the Total Office Environment," May 21, 1979.

IES Lighting Handbook, 5th ed., New York: Illuminating Engineering Society, 1972.

Illuminating Engineering, "Visual Discomfort Ratings for Interior Lighting: Report 2," prepared by Sub-Committee on Direct Glare, Committee on Recommendations for Quality and Quantity of Illumination, 61, No. 10 (1966), pp. 643-666.

Kokoscha, S. and P. Haubner, "Luminance Ratios at Visual Display Workstations and Work Performance," *Abstracts: International Scientific Conference on Ergonomic and Health Aspects in Modern Offices,* Turin, Italy, Nov. 7-9, 1983, p. 68.

LeFort, R.J., "Furniture-Integrated Task/Ambient Lighting," *Interior Design,* Feb. 1978.

McCormack, P., "Take It Straight from the Sun: Get More Light in Your Diet," *Extra,* Continental Airlines, May, 1980, pp. 28-32.

McCormick, E.J., *Human Factors in Engineering and Design*, 4th ed., New York: McGraw-Hill Inc., 1976.

Marquard, R.J., "Energy-Efficient Office Lighting," *The Office*, Sept., 1977.

Morton, Alvin H., article in *Administrative Management*, November, 1982, p. 41.

Nuckolls, James L., "Illuminations," *Interiors*, June, 1981.

Shellko, P.L. and H.G. Williams, "Integration of Task and Ambient Lighting in Furniture," *Lighting Design and Application*, Sept. 1976.

Shemitz, S.R., "Furniture — Integrated Task/Ambient Lighting," *Interior Design*, Feb. 1978.

Wells, B.W.P., "Subjective Responses to the Lighting Installation in a Modern Office Building and Their Design Implications," *Building Science*, 1, SFB:Ab7:UDC 628.9777 (1965), pp. 57-68.

Chapter Five
ACOUSTICS

Technology has roared noisily into the modern office. In the Steelcase/Harris survey mentioned earlier, office workers indicated that their ability to concentrate in the presence of noise and other distractions has a strong effect on how well they do their jobs. But there is inconclusive evidence as to whether moderate noise levels affect general work performance. There is no concrete evidence to date concerning the adverse effects of general noise levels on reaction time, on the learning of simple tasks, or on the results of intelligence and coordination tests. There are, however, indications that certain noises may affect performance on complex tasks calling for vigilance (Broadbent 1958, Jerison 1959), skill and speed (Roth 1968), a high level of perceptual capacity (Boggs and Simon 1968), and complex psychomotor tasks (Eschenbrenner 1971).

Recent research also indicates that how we perceive noise depends upon our attitudes as well as on decibel level. The degree of irritation people feel appears to vary greatly depending upon how predictable the noise is and how necessary it seems to be. Evidence also suggests that noise can reduce a person's sociability and sensitivity to the needs of others (Cohen 1981).

While the effects on work performance are not fully established, the annoyance characteristics of some sounds and their ability to disturb concentration are well known to anyone working in today's offices. Figure 5-1 (Kaplan 1978) illustrates typical office sound levels.

86 Acoustics

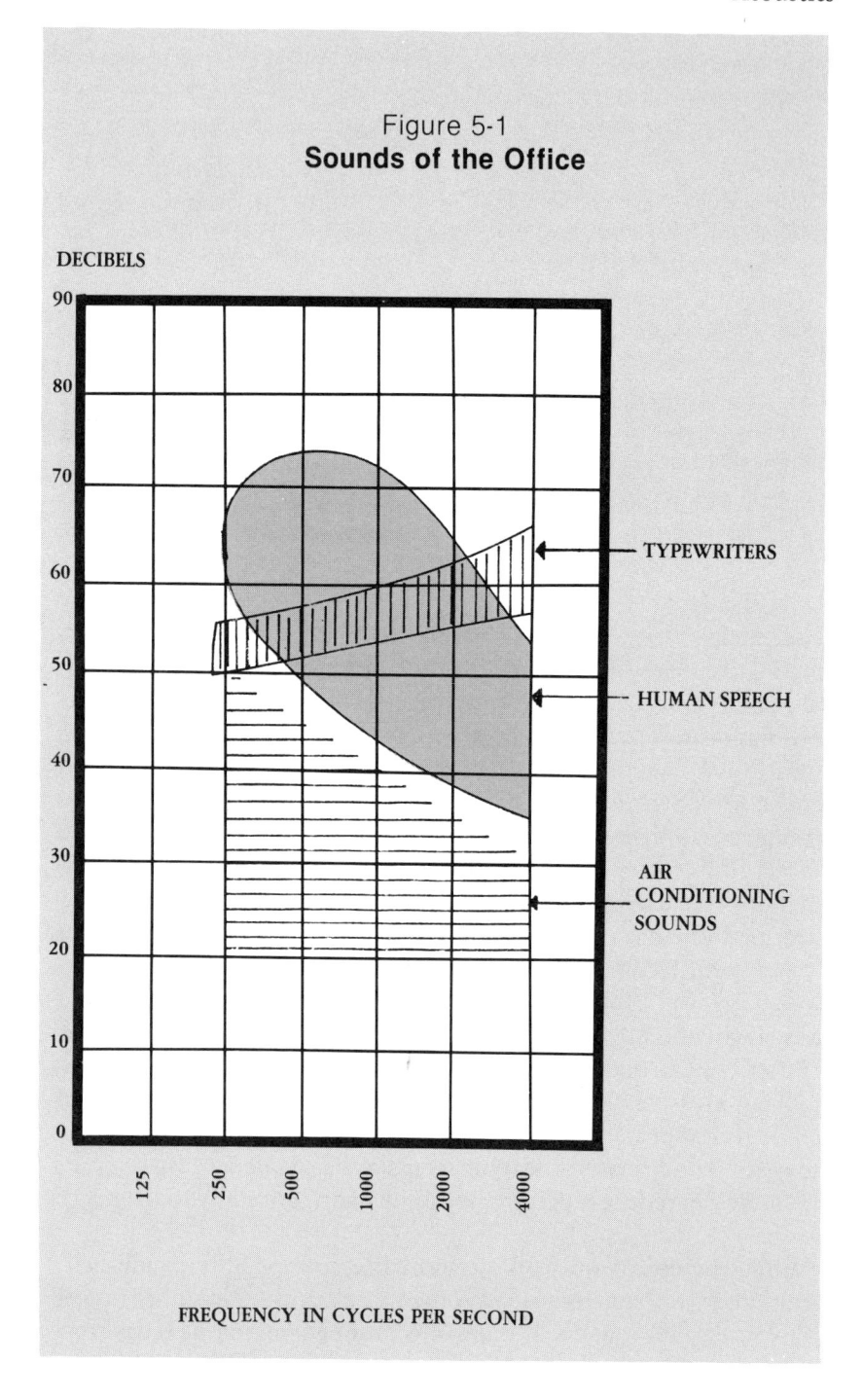

Figure 5-1
Sounds of the Office

← TYPEWRITERS

← HUMAN SPEECH

← AIR CONDITIONING SOUNDS

FREQUENCY IN CYCLES PER SECOND

Acoustics

The sound generated by human speech approaches 80 decibels. Most teleprinters, word processors, and typewriters produce sounds in the 60-to-80 decibel range. Each doubling of a noise source increases the noise level by three decibels. A collection of office machinery operating in a single office can quickly raise the noise level to unsatisfactory limits. Relaxed conversation is usually possible below 45 decibels. Telephone conversations become difficult at about 55 decibels, and one has to shout to be heard at 80 decibels.

To prevent health hazards, the government has established upper limits for acoustic noise, as summarized in Table 5-1. These standards are much too high for an office, however.

Sound levels above 60 decibels in offices are generally considered noisy. According to Kaplan (1978), high noise levels in offices can cause such physiological and psychological effects as increased blood pressure, accelerated heart rate, increased metabolic rate and muscular tension, decreased digestive activity, tension, mental stress, irritability, and inability to think and work efficiently.

Sound has an attention-getting quality and usually competes for a person's attention. It may be perceived as either pleasant, neutral, or unpleasant. Unpleasant sounds are generally considered to be noise, but defining sound quality is difficult and is more an aesthetic problem than an objective science. For humans, sound possesses the characteristics of absence, frequency, adaptation, and variety.

Table 5-1
U.S. Government Standards for Exposure to Sound

Maximum Hours Exposure Per Day	Sound Level (Decibels)
8	90
6	92
4	95
3	97
2	100
1.5	102
1	105
0.5	110
0.25 or less	115

Absence. A total lack of sound is disturbing to most people, and can have adverse psychological effects.

Frequency. People react more favorably to continual, steady and rhythmical sounds than to irregular patterns. The irregular timing of some sounds can be distressing.

Adaptation. Because the hearing mechanism adapts to sound levels, people condition themselves to an existing acoustical environment, be it good or bad. Several degrees of change, for better or worse, can be accepted, but radical change in either direction can be psychologically upsetting.

Variety. A variety of sounds is necessary to maintain sensory alertness and interest.

Acoustical Privacy

A major sound source in the office is people. The distracting effects of overheard conversations can be devastating to concentration. In office design, the ability to hear coworkers' conversations at adjacent workstations is not as important as whether the conversation is understood. Awareness of the conversation may exist, but its content should not be discernible.

Freedom from the distracting influences of noise and overheard conversations is called *acoustical privacy.* A measure of acoustical privacy is the articulation index, which indicates the percentage of words coming from an adjacent workstation that can be understood when the speaker is using a conversational voice. Figure 5-2 illustrates the articulation index. Confidential privacy in offices generally requires an articulation index of five percent or less, while normal privacy requires at least 20 percent.

Noise Control

The objective of an office acoustics program is to keep sound and noise levels within a range that is comfortable for performing human office activities. Those levels should eliminate distractions, allow good hearing, and provide speech privacy.

In planning a noise control program, the primary consideration is the source of unwanted sound. Sound radiates in an expanding spherical wave. As waves hit various objects (ceilings, walls, furniture, people), they may be absorbed or reflected, depending on the kind of

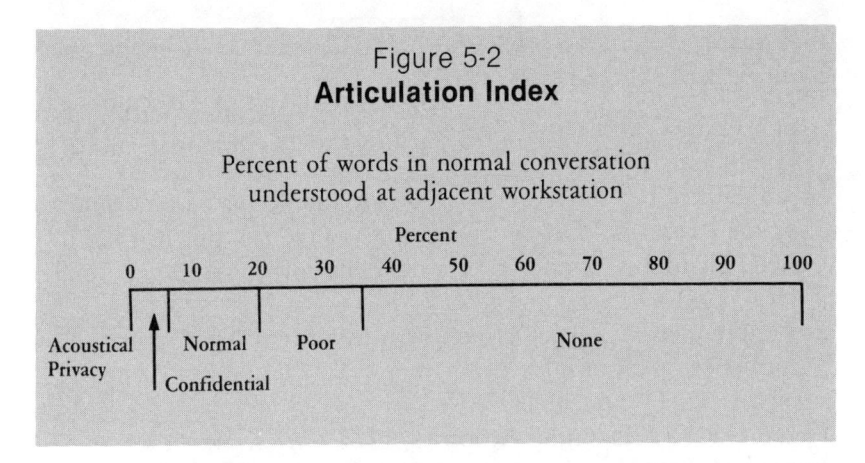

Acoustics

Figure 5-2
Articulation Index

Percent of words in normal conversation understood at adjacent workstation

| 0 | 10 | 20 | 30 | 40 | 50 | 60 | 70 | 80 | 90 | 100 |

Acoustical Privacy — Normal / Confidential — Poor — None

material they encounter. The objective of acoustical design should be to minimize sound-reflective surfaces so that sounds diminish quickly, according to the laws of physics (five to six decibels per doubling of distance).

Some sounds, like the human voice, are directional in nature — when people speak, the sound waves travel mainly in front. A design objective should be to channel these sounds in directions that cause the least disturbance.

An effective noise-control program focuses on three areas: the use of sound-absorbent materials, a sound-masking system, and office layout.

Sound-absorbent materials. Such materials are used on walls and furniture, and it is critical that they be used on ceilings.

Sound-masking systems. These eliminate the startling effects of sporadic noise. When a correctly adjusted sound-masking system is first installed, people are usually aware not of the new sound, but of a quieter workspace (Turley 1978). Music or nature sounds combined with random-pattern noise, however, can exacerbate undesirable noise (Young and Berry 1979).

Office layout. Barriers and desks should be located so that workers are not in the path of voice or machine sounds. People walking past workstations are major sources of disturbance.

Specific guidelines for noise control are included in the next chapter on office design and layout. For more detailed discussions of acoustics, see Herbert (1978) and Turley (1978). Like lighting, acoustics is extremely complex and technical, and an extensive sound-control program should not be undertaken without expert guidance.

REFERENCES

Boggs, D.H. and J.R. Simon, "Differential Effect of Noise on Tasks of Varying Complexity," *Journal of Applied Psychology*, 52. No. 2 (1968), pp. 148-153.

Broadbent, D.E., "Effect of Noise on an 'Intellectual' Task," *Journal of the Acoustical Society of America*, 30 (1958), pp. 824-827.

Cohen, Sheldon, "Sound Effects on Behavior," *Psychology Today*, Oct., 1981.

Eschenbrenner, A.J. Jr., "Effects of Intermittent Noise on the Performance of a Complex Psychomotor Task," *Human Factors*, 13, No. 1 (1971), pp. 59-63.

Herbert, R.K., "Planning Acoustics," *The Office*, March 1978.

Jerison, H.J., "Effects of Noise on Human Performance," *Journal of Applied Psychology*, 43 (1959), pp. 96-101.

Kaplan, A., "An Ergonomic Approach to Acoustics," *Modern Office Procedures*, March, 1978.

Roth, E.M., ed., *Compendium of Human Responses to the Aerospace Environment*, Nov., 1968, NASA CR-1205.

Turley, A.M., "Acoustical Privacy for the Open Office," *The Office*, May, 1978.

Young, H.H. and G.L. Berry, "The Impact of Environment on the Productivity Attitudes of Intellectually Challenged Office Workers," *Human Factors*, 21, No. 4 (1979), pp. 399-407.

Chapter Six
OFFICE DESIGN AND LAYOUT

Workstations must ultimately be integrated into the total office environment. The manner in which this is done can have a significant impact on human performance. A variety of factors are involved, ranging from office layout, distraction control, color, and climate to some unique considerations imposed by the use of VDTs.

The Open Office

The trend today is toward the open office — a large room usually containing 20 or more people that is functionally organized and landscaped with temporary walls, dividers, or plants. The primary advantages of this approach are: economy (more usable floor space: Schmid 1967); a more favorable work environment (light, acoustics and climate: Einbrodt and Beckmann 1969); and organizational benefits (increased flexibility in reorganization, quicker communications and easier information exchange: Kyburz 1968). Strong arguments against the open office include psychosocial factors, such as decreased personal interest in the working sphere and difficulty in integrating into large groups (Heusser 1968), and susceptibility to visual and auditory distractions.

There is little evidence to indicate whether the open office improves or impairs productivity. Most current data focuses on attitudes toward the concept. McCarrey *et al* (1974) found that the open approach resulted in positive attitudes toward job satisfaction, communication effectiveness, and high productivity. Negative attitudes pointed to a lack of visual and auditory privacy, inability to communicate confidentially, poor territorial definitions, and less freedom.

Nemecek and Grandjean (1973), in a study of Swiss offices, found that perceived advantages of the open office included better communication (48 percent); personal contacts (28 percent); and workflow, supervision and discipline (15 percent). Primary disadvantages were: disturbance in concentration (69 percent) and impossibility of confidential conversations (11 percent). Acoustical distractions were the most frequent cause of disturbed concentration. Other relevant findings were that almost two-thirds of the workers thought the large office space was more efficient and more practical, and almost the same proportion of those initially disagreeable to the open office concept later indicated they had adjusted to it.

Turley (1978) has attributed the failure of many open office plans to hard ceilings that increase the spread of sound and reflect it over the tops of partial-height barriers. Others argue that neither the open office nor the traditional office has yet solved the problem of the person who needs high levels of both personal interaction and privacy.

It is still being debated whether or not the trend toward the open office is continuing. Trade associations report that open office furniture sales have grown at twice the rate of conventional furniture in recent years and that about 50 percent of the white-collar workforce is employed in open offices. They estimate that the open office utilization ratio will widen to three to one in the next decade. Other experts claim the trend is swinging back to offices with walls and doors. Whichever is correct, it appears that the open office is here to stay, and office automation will have to settle comfortably into it.

Elements

Building requirements. The open office, if it is to truly reflect the changing needs of people, must be placed in a building that is technically capable of handling it. Adams *et al* (1979) described the building-related characteristics listed below as those needed to permit the most effective implementation of the open office concept. They state that while interior open office systems can adapt well to most kinds of spaces, too often they are placed in buildings that are poorly designed to accommodate changing requirements. The result is that the

Office Design and Layout

building shell and services become a limiting factor in the ideal application of open office systems. Ultimately, they believe, the evolution toward the open office will determine the form of building envelopes.

Building Requirements of the Open Office

The open office requires a building with these characteristics:
- should have an open block not constrained or inhibited by fixed architectural elements;
- should be rectangular and not excessively irregular, elongated or subject to odd geometrics;
- should have fixed architectural elements (such as toilets, elevators, and stairs) consolidated on the perimeter;
- should include easily accessible chases, raceways, and cavities as an integral part of the building shell.

Office layout. An office layout should accomplish two goals. It should optimize the flow of work between various departments and people, and it should minimize movement and sound distractions caused by people going about their activities.

Office Layout

The following principles should determine office layouts:
- keep people close to those with whom they must frequently communicate;
- keep files and other references close to the people who use them;
- keep people who have many outside visitors close to the work area entrance;
- common destinations (toilets, elevators, photocopy machines, and so on) should be close together and accessible by direct routes;
- workstations should be away from sources of intermittent sounds and areas of frequent conversations.

Terminal locations. If a terminal is not located on a person's desk (and is of the regional or satellite variety), its location can greatly affect its usage. Evidence indicates that the distance between a device and its users is a critical factor in its utilization, particularly when it must be shared or reserved in advance (Reid 1973).

Care must be taken in terminal placement so as not to disrupt the social patterns of the office. Systems have failed in the past because terminal operators were isolated from colleagues (Heffernan 1979).

Terminals should also permit visual and auditory privacy because many people, especially those in more prestigious positions, do not want to feel foolish in front of their peers or subordinates. They are prepared to use a terminal only if their mistakes will not be observed. Managers and other untrained users must not be put in a position in which someone else is looking over their shoulders. Even a skilled user would find it difficult to think creatively under such circumstances.

Terminal Locations

- Terminals must be conveniently located and immediately accessible to users.
- For professional and managerial use, terminal placement should permit visual and auditory privacy.

Controlling visual and acoustic distractions. Even an ideal office layout cannot eliminate distracting influences in the work environment, since people must communicate and occasionally move around. Control of the distracting influence of these activities is best accomplished through treatment of the office environment.

Acoustical planning is a complicated subject involving many factors, such as the materials composing ceilings, walls, floors, and barriers, where people are located, and how far apart people are. The guidelines here are simply intended to point out possible distraction problems and to suggest ways of controlling them. Herbert (1978), Kaplan (1978) and Turley (1978) provide thorough discussions of acoustic programs.

Effective sound-absorbent material must be at least one-half inch thick and have a porous surface. It should also have a high absorption coefficient (the percent of sound absorbed).

Barriers are one good method of blocking sound transmission and preventing visual distractions. Turley (1978) found that the optimum barrier height is six feet. A four-foot barrier was found to be useless, while a five-foot one was twice as effective as the four-foot barrier for many applications. Optimum barrier lengths depend on the needs of the work area.

Office Design and Layout

A highly sound-absorbent ceiling is the most important component of an open office plan. A ceiling's absorption coefficient at important speech frequencies should be 0.85 or higher. Ceilings rated below 0.8 are inferior. Ceiling height should be at least nine feet.

Vertical surfaces adjacent to workstations can be as important as ceilings. Sound-absorbent panels can be placed on these walls or columns. The most critical area is from desktop height to six feet above the floor.

A major sound reflector is the large flat lens covering many ceiling light fixtures. Louvered or egg-crate diffusers can sometimes help eliminate strong reflections.

In office layout, the position of overhead lighting fixtures in relation to workstations should be coordinated to avoid annoying sound reflections. Task lighting can alleviate these problems.

Most carpets are acoustically ineffective since they are thin and, on the average, absorb only about 10 to 30 percent of the sound energy hitting them. Their major advantage is that they reduce impact noise caused by footsteps, scraping chairs and falling objects.

Plants offer no acoustical advantage at all, but they do make the work area more pleasant.

Windows create difficult acoustical problems. The desire to see outside and the need to control sound reflections are usually not compatible. An effective compromise is to angle windows slightly outward at the top so that the sound energy is reflected toward a sound-absorbent ceiling. Other less effective solutions for stopping window sound-reflections include vertical venetian blinds with adjustable angles.

Controlling Visual and Acoustic Distractions

- Use barriers to block sound transmissions and prevent visual distractions. Barriers should be at least five feet (preferably six feet) high and should go to the floor.
- Use efficient sound-absorbent materials with high absorption coefficients for ceilings (most important) and for barriers and walls. For walls, the most important area is from desktop height to six feet above the floor.
- Position overhead lights to minimize sound reflected from the lens material to workstations.

- Angle windows slightly outward at the top so that sound energy is reflected toward the sound-absorbent ceiling.
- Consider using supplemental sound-absorbing baffles.
- Use a noise-masking system so that there is no more than a continuous, unobtrusive, indistinguishable murmur throughout the workspace.

Climate. Climate conditions can influence performance, depending on an individual's stress and energy levels and the time period over which work is performed. Table 6-1 describes some general temperature and ventilation considerations. No absolute or simple rules exist. Wing (1965) analyzed the results of a number of studies concerning mental performance and heat, and identified temperatures which, with different exposure times, caused decreased performance.

Table 6-1
Climate Considerations

Temperature
- Personal preferences may vary up to 15° for the same job and conditions.
- Females often prefer higher skin temperatures than males.
- The comfort range is often only about 8°F between too cool and too warm.
- Higher humidity (above 80%) requires 3° to 5°F lower temperature for comfort than lower humidity.
- High muscle activity can reduce the preferred air temperature by 30°F.
- Short sleeves and light clothing requires 5° to 10°F higher temperature than long sleeves and medium clothing for comfort.
- Preferred temperatures vary slightly with outdoor temperatures: cooler in winter and warmer in summer.
- Still air feels warmer than moving air.
- Warm or cold areas (walls, floors, etc.) can affect comfort, even if air temperature is ideal.

Ventilation
- Drafts from fans and ventilators can be very annoying and even intolerable to some people.

Office Design and Layout

The upper limit for unimpaired mental performance began in the mid-80s (Fahrenheit) for exposure periods from four to five hours, and reached the following approximate points: 90 degrees for two hours exposure, and 95 degrees for one hour. Generally speaking, comfort levels are lower than those at which performance begins to deteriorate (McCormick 1976).

Carlton-Foss (1982) reports that performance drops about 50 percent when the temperature increases 11 degrees, or decreases seven degrees, from the central temperature at which a person performs best.

Optimally, temperatures should be maintained within desirable ranges. The electrical components of VDTs generally produce a certain amount of waste heat. It is estimated that the heat generated by one VDT is equivalent to that generated by one person. Thus in an office where each worker has a VDT at his or her workstation, the additional heat created is equal to that of doubling the workforce in the room.

Office ventilation is becoming an increasingly volatile topic. In addition to eliminating drafts from fans and ventilators, pollutants from cigarette smoke and other office materials should be effectively removed, not just recirculated.

To eliminate environmental pollution, Wanner (1983) recommends that the fresh air supply should be sufficient to prevent the carbon dioxide content from exceeding 0.15 percent. To achieve this goal in a non-smoking environment, 12 to 15 cubic meters of fresh air per person per hour are necessary. If smoking is present, 30 to 40 cubic meters of fresh air per person per hour may be required.

Cigar smoking should be confined to sealed offices or to places with direct access to outside air. Many who object to cigar smoke will simply not get used to it. For a thorough discussion of energy engineering, see Carlton-Foss (1982).

Climate

Temperature and Humidity
- Maintain room temperatures between 68 and 76 degrees.
- Maintain relative humidity between 40 and 60 percent.

Ventilation
- Provide sufficient fresh air.
- Eliminate drafts from fans and ventilators.

Color. Color affects our moods, out attitudes and our feelings of comfort. If used properly it can enhance our performance, creating a positive, satisfying environment. It is one of the softer aspects of design called *high-touch* that John Naisbitt defines in his book, *Megatrends,* as countermeasures to *high-tech.* These countermeasures are adopted to balance the pervasive effects of technology on our lives.

The psychological and physiological effects of color on people are described in Table 6-2 (from Digerness 1982) and Table 6-3 (from Beach 1973).

Table 6-2
Effects of Color

Red
- Overstimulates and increases blood pressure
- Creates feelings of warmth

Black and Brown
- Create feelings of fatigue
- Decrease perception of light

White
- Produces no strong reactions
- Increases perception of light and space

Blue
- Relaxing — reduces blood pressure and the effects of stress
- Overuse can cause sluggish behavior
- Perceived as cold

Yellow
- No effect on blood pressure
- Can cause eyestrain if too bright or overused
- Perceived as warm
- Can stimulate a cheerful mood
- Highest retention rating of all colors

Green
- Considered the most normal color
- No abnormal reactions
- Can have a sedative effect
- May be perceived as cool or cold

Office Design and Layout

Table 6-3
Physiological and Psychological Effects of Color

Condition	Worst	Best
Fatiguing	Red, Orange, Yellow	Light tints (buff, ivory, cream, pale yellow, pale green)
Reading Speed	Red and blue backgrounds	Black on white, Black on yellow
Preferences		Blue, red, green
Emotional Reactions:		
Stimulating		Red, orange
Restful/Depressing		Blue, violet, Blue-green

Bright colors are fatiguing because the human eye reacts to the volume of light entering it. Bright colors make the pupil contract, and since the action is muscular, the eyes tire when a shift is made from this brightness to surrounding dull colors.

Human-response time to color signals has been measured from fastest to slowest as: red, green, yellow and white. Any bright signal that has a good contrast ratio against a dark background, however, has good attention-getting qualities (Reynolds *et al* 1972).

Selecting a color or colors for use in an office depends upon a variety of factors. These include the following considerations.
- What work functions will take place? Formal? Informal?
- Where is the area located in relation to the rest of the building? In sunlight? Exposed to outdoor light? Under artificial light?
- What effect is to be achieved? To stimulate? To relax?

Digerness (1982) provides an interesting discussion of the use of color in today's offices. The understanding and proper use of colors can contribute greatly to the subjective quality of the office environment as well as alleviating reported eye discomforts associated with using VDTs.

Other factors. To provide relief for the eyes of one who has to spend a large part of the day in close work with a VDT and source materials, restroom facilities should be restfully decorated, well-lighted, and have no strong contrasts of lightness and shade, or stillness and movement. This will provide a restful diversion for the eye mechanism. Workstation design should also permit, where possible, a horizon beyond the VDT where the eyes can focus on a tranquilizing background.

The effect of background music on the office worker is conflicting. For creative, mentally challenging tasks, it does not appear to be beneficial. For repetitive tasks, positive results have been reported. Nemecek (1983), in a study of Swiss bank employees' reactions to background music, found that about two-thirds of the employees interviewed felt that it improves the working environment. Managers and senior staff were disturbed twice as much as other employees, and disturbances increased with higher education and age. Light music was found to be considerably less annoying than classical or pop music.

REFERENCES

Adams, J., C. Nuttall and R. Propst, *The Integrated Office Facility,* Ann Arbor, MI: Herman Miller Research Corp., June, 1979.

Beach, T., "Color in Paperwork," *The Office,* May, 1973, pp. 80-86.

Carlton-Foss, John A., "Energy Engineering for Occupied Places," ASHRAE Journal, Oct., 1982, pp. 35-39.

Digerness, Bobbi, "Color It Productive," *Administrative Management,* December, 1982, pp. 46-49.

Einbrodt, H.J. and H. Beckmann, "Luft-, Licht- und Lärmproblem in Klein- und Grossraumbüros," *Arbeitsmedizin Sozialmedizin Arbeitshygiene,* 2 (1969), pp. 49-52.

Heffernan, J., of American Mutual Insurance Companies, Wakefield, MA, Personal Conversation, Oct., 1979.

Herbert, R.K., "Planning Acoustics," *The Office,* March, 1978.

Heusser, M., "Psychologische Aspekte des Grossraumbüros." *Büro und Verkauf,* 37 (1968) pp. 452-457.

Kaplan, A., "An Ergonomic Approach to Acoustics." *Modern Office Procedures,* March, 1978.

Kyburz, W., "Der Grossraum als organisatorisches Ideal," *Büro und Verkauf,* 37 (1968), pp. 433-435.

McCormick, E.J., *Human Factors in Engineering and Design*, 4th ed., New York: McGraw-Hill Inc., 1976.

McCarrey, M.W., L. Peterson, S. Edwards and P. Von Kulmiz, "Landscape Office Attitudes: Reflections of Perceived Degree of Control Over Transactions with the Environment," *Journal of Applied Psychology*, 59 (1974), pp. 401-403.

Nemecek, J., "Music During Office Work," *Abstracts: International Scientific Conference on Ergonomic and Health Aspects in Modern Offices*, Turin, Italy, Nov. 7-9, 1983, p. 39.

Nemecek J., and E. Grandjean, "Results of an Ergonomics Investigation of Large-Space Offices," *Human Factors*, 15, No. 2 (1973), pp. 111-124.

Reid, A.A.L., "Channel Versus System Innovation Person/Person Telecommunications," *Human Factors*, 15, No. 5 (1973), pp. 449-457.

Reynolds, R.E., R.M. White Jr. and R.L. Hilgendorf, "Detection and Recognition of Colored Signal Lights," *Human Factors*, 14, No. 3 (1972), pp. 227-236.

Schmid, R., "Der mittelgrosse Büroraum." *Industrielle Organisation*, 36 (1967), pp. 348-356.

Turley, A.M., "Acoustical Privacy for the Open Office," *The Office*, May, 1978.

Wanner, H.U., "Indoor Air Quality in Offices," *Abstracts: International Scientific Conference on Ergonomic and Health Aspects in Modern Offices*, Turin, Italy. Nov. 7-9, 1983, p. 16.

Wing, J.F., *A Review of the Effects of High Ambient Temperature on Mental Performance*, USAF, AMRL, TR 65-102, Sept., 1965.

Chapter Seven
TELECOMMUTING

A centralized place of work is a relatively recent phenomenon. For 10,000 years people labored in their own cottages and fields, moving to the factory only when the division of labor promised increased productivity. Cheap energy, a relatively low value on personal time, and difficulties in moving and storing information sustained this direction for more than two centuries.

Today, however, energy is no longer cheap, personal time has greater human value, and paper as a medium of information exchange and storage is being replaced by electronics. Coupled with the high cost of workspace and its inefficient use (the typical office is fully staffed only one-third of the time), the necessity and desirability of a centralized office is greatly reduced. Why not move the workplace to the home? After all, many homes remain empty precisely the same hours the office is full.

Thus the concept of telecommuting has emerged, extending the traditional office into the confines of one's personal living space. It is really not such a rash idea at all — many professional workers have blended home and work for years as have those who have surrounded themselves at the kitchen table in the evening with "...a few things I brought home from the office."

Estimates of the percentage of office workers who could telecommute range as high as 50 percent. Telecommuting has awesome benefits, but it also has frightening sociological and behavioral implications, as outlined in Table 7-1.

Table 7-1
Advantages and Disadvantages of Telecommuting

Advantages
- Increases productivity by:
  1. creating a longer workday;
  2. permitting activities when the inspiration arises;
  3. eliminating disruptions and distractions;
  4. reducing non-availability times.

- Expands available workforce by:
  1. removing geographical restrictions in employment;
  2. providing flexibility;
  3. tapping home-bound labor force.

- Reduces operating and overhead costs
- Conserves energy
- Creates more personal time

Disadvantages
- Isolation caused by:
  1. lack of social contacts;
  2. absence of feedback;
  3. absence of idea fertilization.

- Professional anonymity
- Blurring of distinction between home and work
- Management acceptance
- Difficulties in measuring productivity
- Legal, logistical and personnel problems

Advantages

Increases productivity. Telecommuting frees one from the tyranny of time, transportation and location. The workday can begin five minutes after the worker rises from bed, and end five minutes before retiring. It is common in many large metropolitan areas to spend one to two hours commuting each way to the office. At home, work can be accomplished when the worker is inspired, even at 2:00 a.m. The disruptions and distractions of the busy office disappear. People are available when they previously were not, such as during commuting, after hours, or during out-of-town business trips.

Expands available workforce. The ability to hire and retain employees for many of today's highly competitive office jobs is increased. Eliminating geographical restrictions and providing work flexibility are important factors to many potential and existing workers. The home-bound labor force is also made available. Mothers of young children, the aged, or the handicapped are easily utilized.

Reduces overhead and operating costs. Office space, and the costs associated with it, are reduced. So are those involving employee relocation.

Conserves energy. Consumption of transportation fuel, and fuels used in heating and cooling the office, are greatly reduced. The impact on automobile gasoline consumption could be dramatic — a savings of more than 300,000 barrels a day. A person decreasing driving by 500 miles per month could save $50 to $100 each month.

Creates more personal time. The worker will benefit through the creation of more personal time. Former commuting time can be used to fulfill personal needs such as recreation, hobbies, leisure, or just being with the family.

Disadvantages

Isolation. People are social creatures, and to many, the work experience is a social outlet. The coffee klatch or just plain gossip can be stimulating and refreshing. For many workers, the social organization of the workplace is a means of enhancing self-esteem and of satisfying needs for companionship, affiliation and belonging (Harvey 1967). The social atmosphere of the office also satisfies a need for those looking for a mate.

We also need the physical presence of others to share in the nonverbal forms of communication which make us truly human, visible and real to each other. The presence of others is reassuring, and feedback is a much-needed commodity. The spontaneity and richness of human-to-human communication is impossible when working in isolation.

One company that implemented an electronic mail system found that messages from remote workers demonstrated gradually increasing anxiety and misunderstanding. Their messages eventually became paranoid. The company found that when the workers reached that point, it was best to temporarily bring them back to the work society. Thus, it appears that eliminating social feedback may have a critical impact on some people. Imagine sitting in the office for weeks and never seeing another soul.

Cross-fertilization of ideas is also lacking. Since we learn from each other, isolation inhibits professional development. For some, visibility within the office is the key to getting ahead.

Blurring of distinction between home and work. Home to many is the refuge from the trials and tribulations of work. The work personality is formal and less personal; that in the home less formal and warmer. What are the implications of carrying the work personality home — of continuous proximity to one's spouse — of continuing visibility of one's office? Will domestic roles — as parents, wives or husbands — interfere with jobs? Will jobs interfere with domestic roles? Some suggest that the result will be increased stress and a strain on marriages. Forced proximity may not guarantee happiness. Spillover of work-related issues into the home may not be healthy.

Interruptions and distractions of a different sort may occur. Schedules may have to be shuffled to meet family demands (e.g. the garbage collector always comes on Thursday afternoon). Interruptions of well-meaning people under three feet tall, and shaggy critters with wagging tails, may have to be fended off, thereby satisfying neither the goals of work life nor family life. Powers of self-discipline may be severely tested.

Management acceptance. Managers see their presence in the office as necessary for direction, motivation and morale (Carne 1972). Many are accustomed to having armies of people under observation and control. They are trained to supervise people who sit and look like they are working hard. Eight hours a desk equates to eight hours of work. A common management attitude is that people who work at home are not working.

The work of many executives, managers and employees is directly concerned with interpersonal communication, most of it face to face. Evidence already presented indicates that technologically mediated communications are not conducive to many interpersonal relationships.

Difficulties in measuring productivity. How can the telecommuting worker be monitored? How can productivity be measured? Are specific outputs and deliverables a desirable criteria? Is invisible monitoring through the terminal acceptable? This, of course, conjures up images of "Big Brother."

Legal, logistical and personnel problems. Telecommuting is not without its share of legal, logistical and other personnel problems. Manning (1981), in describing Control Data Corporation's working-at-home program, mentions a few.

Legal questions are associated with state and Federal regulations as well as corporate policies and procedures, and include:

- security of equipment;
- privacy of customer information;
- municipal ordinances and neighborhood businesses;
- insurance (both theft and liability);
- eligibility and selection criteria as related to home accommodations;
- tax matters;
- worker's compensation insurance limitations.

Logistical problems include:

- determining scheduling and long-range facility requirements;
- selecting equipment to support remote employees;
- supplying office materials, telephones, etc.;
- distribution of internal and external communications and mail, job postings, etc.;
- provision of clerical and secretarial support.

Additional personnel problems to be addressed include:

- providing satisfactory formal meetings and informal communications;
- eligibility and selection criteria for home work assignments;
- education and training;
- employee/labor relations issues.

These are but a few of a large set of problems that must be confronted. A successful telecommuting program must address them all.

Experimental Telecommuting Programs

Many organizations, among them Control Data Corporation, Mountain Bell of Colorado, and the Continental Illinois National Bank of Chicago, have installed pilot telecommuting projects. So far, the results are mixed. Control Data Corp. (Manning 1981) found self-rated increases in productivity of 12 to 20 percent. The supervisors of telecommuting workers agreed with these self-ratings. CDC believes that one day increases as high as 200 to 300 percent in some jobs will be possible. Mountain Bell reports increases from 50 to 150 percent (Rifkin 1982). A study conducted at Cornell University (McClintock 1982) found that telecommuting resulted in an overall increase in the output of complex, non-routine work.

On the other hand, Continental Illinois Bank's program, begun in 1978, was terminated in late 1982 because it was not cost effective. Too many people were involved in getting information to the home and then back to bank officials needing to see it.

In interpreting the results of these studies it must be kept in mind that the participants were selected people performing selected jobs. The issues are complicated and situations are specific to each employer. What might succeed for one company might not work for another. Much still remains to be learned.

Telecommuting Guidelines and Implications

Control Data Corporation has found a number of factors influencing the success of telecommuting projects. First, the worker must want to telecommute. People who have the option of choosing the work location that best suits their personal or work needs will be more motivated at the location they choose. One problem is that often people simply do not know if they will like working at a remote site. Next, the task must be conducive to being performed outside the regular office. Enough still is not known about which tasks and jobs best fit telecommuting. Plentiful communication to telecommuters is also necessary. The worker must be made to feel a part of the group. Finally, management and others who do not choose to telecommute must understand and support the concept.

Satellite offices (neighborhood offices scattered about the metropolitan area containing the main office) may yield the best of both worlds for the telecommuting worker. While maintaining many of the advantages of working at home (shorter commute, more free time, etc.), it eliminates some of the most severe disadvantages (isolation and blurring of distinction between work and home). Some feel, however, that this approach would be costly (Manning 1981) unless the facility is shared among other organizations. If so, it may still limit the learning experiences that the availability of professional peers provides.

On a longer-term basis, telecommuting has implications which can impact the structure of work, the organization, lifestyles and society. Some of these were first presented by Albertson (1977), and are outlined in Table 7-2 and below.

Loosening of the nine-to-five workday structure. Work will no longer be confined to traditional working hours. Work and leisure pursuits will provide a more balanced week. Queuing and crowding currently associated with weekend activities will diminish as levelling throughout the week occurs.

Reduced employee affiliation with work. The corporate logo above the office entrance will no longer be visible, nor will the visually obvious reminders scattered throughout the building of who pays the check. Because job changes will not require physical moves, higher turnover may result.

Greater flexibility in living location. The physical proximity of one's residence to one's job will no longer be important. Convenience to public transportation or good roads will no longer be necessary. Replacing these will be convenience for personal, recreational or avocational reasons. Small towns, rural locations, and good-weather areas will be in much greater demand.

Table 7-2
Long-Term Implications of Telecommuting

- Loosening of nine-to-five workday structure
- Reduced employee affiliation with work
- Greater flexibility in living location
- More fluid employment situation
- More flexible organizations
- Restructuring of personal relationships and lifestyles
- Restructuring of the home

More fluid employment situation. Using hours as a basis of payment will be difficult, and people may have to work under short-term contracts, with payment predicated on project completion. Changing jobs will be as easy as dialing a new telephone number on Monday morning.

More flexible organizations. Without having to provide for the accommodation of an on-site, full-time staff, employers can adjust employee numbers to changing needs and can easily form ad hoc organizations and task forces.

Restructuring of personal relationships and lifestyles. Compatibility of husbands and wives will be tested and possibly reshaped by ongoing proximity. Continuous exposure to each other's job interests and work circumstances can create a greater bond, making it less likely that spouses will grow apart. A sharing of both job work and housekeeping would be possible. A husband and wife could even split a full-time job. Criteria for marriage could expand beyond the traditional bond to include a variety of work-related issues such as responsibility and self-discipline. Children will be able to observe "workday" role models instead of receiving vague descriptions.

Restructuring the home. Houses will get bigger as population densities decrease due to decentralization. Storage needs will increase as fewer shopping trips occur. Work areas may become separately accessible from outside, and inaccessible from the living area to provide a proper balance between the two.

It is clear that while telecommuting offers the potential for reducing administrative costs and boosting productivity, its success depends on thorough planning and monitoring.

REFERENCES

Albertson, L.A., *A Preliminary Report on the Teleconference User Opinion Questionnaire,* Mimeo Australia Post Office, Melbourne, 1974.

Carne, E.B., "Telecommunications: Its Impact on Business," *Harvard Business Review,* 50, No. 4 (1972), pp. 925-933.

Harvey, L.B., "Interpersonal Communication," *Paper Presented at the Annual Conference of the Australian Psychological Society,* 1967.

Manning, R.A., "Alternate Work Site Programs," *Proceedings, Office Technology Research Group*, 1981 Fall Meeting, Williamsburg, VA, Nov., 1981.

McClintock, Charles G., "Study: No Rush to Board Telecommuting Express," *Computerworld.* Jan. 11, 1982, pp. 61-62.

Rifkin, Glenn, "Working Remotely: Where Will Your Office Be?" *Computerworld OA,* 1982.

Chapter Eight
TOWARD THE YEAR 2000

From a vantage point in 1970 one could scarcely have imagined the great impact technology would soon have on the office worker, the office worker's job, and the office environment. Therefore, a look into the future runs the risk of being undermined by the sudden discovery or coming together of a variety of forces in a totally unforeseen way. In order to plan, however, a path must be charted, and the purpose of this chapter is to assist you in doing so. We will look at projected trends and developing technologies and the effect both will have on the office environment as we approach the end of this century.

Human Factors/Ergonomics. Human factors and ergonomic considerations will achieve ever-increasing importance in future environmental design as awareness of their contribution to greater human productivity grows. That this is happening is evidenced by the fact that four of the top five critical problems of office automation that have been identified in the first monograph in this series (Smith 1983) are people-related and can be addressed through application of human factors/ergonomic design principles (see Table 8-1 for summary). That this is happening is also evidenced by the contents of this monograph.

Information. Previously scattered information will be electronically consolidated, thereby reducing the clutter of the workstation. Information will be more accessible to all. Paper will not entirely disappear, however.

Table 8-1
Critical Problems Involving Human Resources and Office Automation*

- **Maintaining a human perspective in automated office settings so that individuals continue to obtain deserved recognition for their accomplishments and are not made to feel controlled by technology.**

  Maintaining a human perspective in the automated office environment is by far the single most critical problem of all those identified in the study. It is obvious from the high degree of criticalness given to this problem that the human resources, or people, factor must come first in an office automation effort. The systems themselves must represent tools to facilitate the work of people.

- **Designing meaningful and satisfying jobs in which employees can succeed in an automated office environment.**

  Generally, designing meaningful and satisfying jobs is seen as quite critical to survey respondents, who are signaling the importance of job design in developing and maintaining an effective office.

- **Ensuring that automated office systems are user and not equipment oriented.**

  All of the respondents except the experts see user orientation to automated office systems as a critical problem.

- **Helping employees who work primarily at terminals to maintain job satisfaction.**

  The significant point here is the employees' *perception* that automated office equipment will require long hours of working at a terminal, which may not be true in many cases. Indeed, automation will result in more creative jobs for some, since it will relieve workers of many routine, manual tasks, permitting more time for new responsibilities and more creative tasks. Thus the employees' perception underscores the need for management to keep employees fully apprised of developments in and advantages of office automation to overcome potential resistance.

* Smith, Harold T., C.A.M., *The Office Revolution: Strategies for Managing Tomorrow's Workforce*, Administrative Management Society Foundation, 1983, pp. 66-68.

Technology. Miniaturization of technology will continue. The bulky CRT display will gradually be replaced by flat-panel displays offering compactness, increased mobility, and the capability of being built into the workstation. Advances in display support electronics will yield improved resolution, color, split-screen capabilities, and three-dimensional perspectives. Larger displays will also be available, permitting the presentation of more information at one time. The typewriter-type keyboard will remain a primary human-computer interface mechanism, but touch-panel displays and pointers such as the mouse and trackballs will have widespread use. Voice recognition and synthesis will be viable in a variety of applications.

Workstations. The workstation of tomorrow will be smaller. Electronic information consolidation will eliminate the need for large areas to store information on paper and the materials needed for paper handling. At the same time, however, greater visual and auditory privacy will be needed. Noise created by equipment and human voice-computer interaction will create severe acoustical problems. Display terminals and other technologies will be incorporated within the workstation itself. The surface of the desk and workstation walls will become control and viewing surfaces. The chair may also contain fingertip controls. The office workstation and the airplane cockpit may bear some resemblance to each other.

Comfort in working will be achieved through intelligent chairs and desks. Desk heights and angles will be modified through the simple touch of a button. Desired configurations will be "remembered" by the desk's electronics and changed as the needs of its occupants change. The chair may actually configure itself to its occupant through analysis of weight distribution.

The office. Office buildings as we know them today will continue to operate. However, a reduction in paper and paper filing requirements and more people working at home or in satellite offices will diminish space requirements. Offices and conference rooms will also still exist. Electronic meetings are a poor substitute for a variety of communications requiring interpersonal interaction. These will best be addressed by people facing people.

Tomorrow's office will provide a computer utility akin to that provided by the electric and telephone companies. A variety of computing services will be available at the touch of a switch.

Some critical concerns. Along with its promise, the technology of tomorrow raises some critical environmental issues that must be addressed. Each will have a significant impact on the well-being of the office worker and the organization. These issues pertain to noise, health, and electronic social isolation.

Noise. Technology has not entered the office quietly. Until now the primary source of decibels and distractions has been the equipment and occasional talking people. As human-computer interaction methods change, and voice communication assumes a greater role in the dialog, a new dimension will be added to the office din. Talking people and talking computers will be an even greater source of distraction and noise than previously. (A visit to a telephone reservation or customer service office, or overheard conversations of coworkers, aptly illustrate the point.) The office of tomorrow will have to face this problem squarely with a much more effective acoustics program than exists today in most organizations. Many offices with open designs could be devastated by the disruptive nature of this new technology.

Health. Tomorrow's jobs must not be made *too* comfortable. The organization of the items making up the workstation and the jobs themselves must facilitate a certain degree of physical movement. The challenge will be to stay on the right side of the line separating healthy diversity from fatigue. Workstation component adjustability will be a key element in achieving this objective. Being able to easily assume a variety of different working postures during the day will provide needed exercise for a range of muscles. Health clubs or exercise rooms may also become integral parts of the office. The coffee break, now used to mentally and physically recharge fatigued minds and bodies, may be supplemented by the exercise break to replenish stiff and rigid bodies.

Social Isolation. The new communication technologies promise us much. Interacting with others through the electronic medium of the computer can improve communication, provide greater interdependence, increase the number of people we deal with, and increase human productivity. But there is another side to this issue. Consider these possibilities:

- The system goes down and you feel helpless and frustrated. You feel ineffectual using the telephone or typewriter.
- Someone calls on the telephone and you are annoyed.
- Someone walks into your office and you are disturbed.
- Computer metaphors such as "message you" and "clear buffer" creep into spoken words.

Unlikely? Not so, say Hiltz and Turoff (1982). Twenty percent of the 500 scientific users of an electronic information exchange system showed these behavioral characteristics. Hiltz and Turoff characterize these people as suffering "network addiction."

Tomorrow's office must provide the proper social environment as well. As we direct more and more of our attention to the computer and structure our workstations around it, the office design must still foster and encourage the human-to-human interactions so vital to us all. The environment must provide the degree of privacy demanded by the new technologies while at the same time not inhibit face-to-face communications.

REFERENCES

Hiltz, Starr Roxanne, and Murray Turoff, in "Users Found Suffering 'Network Addiction,'" *Computerworld,* May 3, 1982, p. 4.

Smith, Harold T., C.A.M., *The Office Revolution: Strategies for Managing Tomorrow's Workforce,* Administrative Management Society Foundation, Willow Grove, PA, 1983.

Chapter 9
Conclusion

The benefits of technology will never be achieved if the technology is not properly assimilated into the office. It is hoped that the environmental guidelines found in the preceding pages will assist this process.

Some of the guidelines found in this monograph have already been incorporated into legislation in several European countries. Some state legislatures, including Illinois and Massachusetts, have had similar bills introduced. Is this a healthy trend? Many experts, among them Ketchel (1982) and Hirsch (1982), as well as this writer, do not think so.

The research base for many of these guidelines is not yet adequate. While many solutions are straightforward and well established, legislation tends to fill in our many knowledge gaps with mandated requirements based upon tenuous research. Inconsistencies in requirements often result. This is evidenced in the review by Rupp (1981) and the disagreements between experts that surfaced at the International Scientific Conference on Ergonomic and Health Aspects in Modern Offices (1983). Even the blind application of reasonably straightforward rules can be dangerous. Many factors interact with one another. We must get a better grasp of all the issues before allowing office automation to enter the legislative arena.

Legislation may also give us a false sense of security, since it implies that the problem is solved — leading to two undesirable outcomes.

One is that much-needed research will be stifled. Another is that research will head in trivial or nonproductive directions, deflecting valuable resources from exploration of the meaningful issues.

Lastly, legislation may impose an unnecessary financial burden on the occasional users of VDTs. Occasional users are not subjected to all the problems described here; to impose solutions to nonproblems is not cost effective. Furthermore, state or Federally mandated requirements necessitate monitoring mechanisms to assure company compliance with the law. This results in tax dollars being spent for solutions of dubious long term value to companies and society, and creates a double curse for users of office computer technology: unnecessary pitfalls and attenuated payoffs.

Psychosocial problems and the physical ailments associated with posture and vision cannot really be neatly divided into separate categories. Nor can the effects of the hardware, the system, the environment, and an organization's management. The worker, too, must be looked upon not just as one but as many with a variety of needs, interests, attitudes and susceptibilities.

A tangible benefit of increased attention to the environment will be increased productivity. Intangible benefits include decreased absenteeism, improved job satisfaction and morale (see Seal and Sylvester 1982), and lowered workers' compensation claims and costs. Humanizing the workplace can also serve as a proactive response to charges by interest groups and organized labor about the health and safety hazards of working with VDTs.

We must not lose sight of the fact that the road to successful implementation of office automation requires harmonization of the worker, the organization, and the technology. The product of our efforts must result in a condition where jobs, computer systems, equipment, the work environment, and the motivations and psychological needs of office workers are properly woven into a whole fabric. Then the process of change must be carefully managed. The results of our efforts will be no stronger than the weakest thread.

REFERENCES

Hirsch, Richard S., "National Standards for the Design of Visual Display Terminals," *Proceedings of the Human Factors Society — 26th Annual Meeting* (1982), Santa Monica, CA, pp. 290-293.

International Scientific Conference on Ergonomic and Health Aspects in Modern Offices, Turin, Italy, November 7-9, 1983.

Ketchel, James, "Human Factors Issues in the Design and Use of Visual Display Terminals (VDTs)," *Office Automation Conference Digest,* San Francisco, CA, April 5-7, 1982.

Rupp, Bruca A., "Visual Display Terminals: A Review of the Issues," *Proceedings of the SID,* Vol. 22, No. 1, 1981.

Seal, Dennis J., and Gordon E. Sylvester, "Design Applications for Optimizing the Working Environment of the Software Employee: A Case Study," *Proceedings of the Human Factors Society — 26th Annual Meeting* (1982), Santa Monica, CA, pp. 150-154.

HF 5547.5 .G36 1984

Galitz, Wilbert O.

The office environment